TECHNOLOGY FOR SEND IN PRIMARY SCHOOLS

Sara Miller McCune founded SAGE Publishing in 1965 to support the dissemination of usable knowledge and educate a global community. SAGE publishes more than 1000 journals and over 800 new books each year, spanning a wide range of subject areas. Our growing selection of library products includes archives, data, case studies and video. SAGE remains majority owned by our founder and after her lifetime will become owned by a charitable trust that secures the company's continued independence.

Los Angeles | London | New Delhi | Singapore | Washington DC | Melbourne

HELEN CALDWELL
STEPHEN CULLINGFORD-AGNEW

TECHNOLOGY FOR SEND IN PRIMARY SCHOOLS

A GUIDE FOR BEST PRACTICE

Learning Matters
An imprint of SAGE Publications Ltd
1 Oliver's Yard
55 City Road
London EC1Y 1SP

SAGE Publications Inc.
2455 Teller Road
Thousand Oaks, California 91320

SAGE Publications India Pvt Ltd
B 1/I 1 Mohan Cooperative Industrial Area
Mathura Road
New Delhi 110 044

SAGE Publications Asia-Pacific Pte Ltd
3 Church Street
#10-04 Samsung Hub
Singapore 049483

Editor: Amy Thornton
Production controller: Chris Marke
Project management: Deer Park Productions
Marketing manager: Lorna Patkai
Cover design: Wendy Scott
Typeset by: C&M Digitals (P) Ltd, Chennai, India
Printed in the UK

Library of Congress Control Number: 2017950168

British Library Cataloguing in Publication Data

A catalogue record for this book is available from the British Library.

ISBN 978-1-5264-0236-3 (pbk)
ISBN 978-1-5264-0235-6

CONTENTS

ABOUT THE AUTHORS AND CONTRIBUTORS

Authors

Helen Caldwell is a Senior Lecturer at the University of Northampton, where she is curriculum lead for primary computing in Teacher Education and programme lead for the Postgraduate Certificate in Primary Computing. Her teaching covers the use of technology across primary subjects, implementing the computing curriculum and assistive technologies for SEND. Helen was a member of the Computing in ITT Expert Group and currently sits on the Association for Information Technology in Teacher Education (ITTE) National Executive Committee. Her research interests include eLearning and social networking in Higher Education, and computing and digital literacy in Primary Education.

Steve Cullingford-Agnew is a Senior Lecturer at the University of Northampton, where he teaches on the BA Hons Special Educational Needs and Inclusion undergraduate course. Teaching includes the undergraduate module Approaches to Support Inclusion through Technology, Postgraduate SEN and Inclusion Master's programmes, and supporting Initial Teacher Education students to gain valuable knowledge and understanding of working within a special school context.

Contributors

Kim Avery is a primary trained teacher working at Billing Brook School, Northampton. She is the computing coordinator at her school and has been actively developing and improving the computing curriculum to ensure that it is both creative and effective. Kim has worked with Barefoot Computing to develop a number of unplugged SEND teaching resources. She has delivered numerous training sessions to promote the use of unplugged computing, including presenting at the BETT Show. Kim is a Computing SLE for Northants as well as being a CAS Master Teacher and Raspberry Pi Certified Educator.

Jean Edwards is a Senior Lecturer in the Faculty of Education and Humanities at the University of Northampton. She has been a teacher, Deputy Head and Headteacher in lower and primary schools. She has an interest in art education, writing *Teaching Primary Art* in 2013 (published by Pearson) and has a developing interest in the potential of digital technology in making art with children. She is a printmaker and urban-sketcher, and takes part in the sketchbook circle, collaborating with other teachers and art educators.

Amy Follows is the Education Manager for Widgit Software, where she trains practitioners to use a wide range of technology to support teaching and learning. Prior to her role at Widgit, she worked in a range of different primary and special school settings. She was Deputy Headteacher within two schools in the Midlands where she led and advanced the literacy and technology strategies. She has always had a passion for using technology to support the primary curriculum, as well as having a particular interest in supporting children with special needs.

John Galloway is a specialist in the use of technology to improve educational inclusion, particularly for children and young people with special educational needs. He works for Tower Hamlets as an advisory teacher, and also as a freelance consultant, trainer and writer. His work covers all phases of schools and learners with a very broad range of SEN. He has spoken at conferences across the UK and internationally, and is widely published as a writer. Most recently, in 2015, he co-authored *Learning with Mobile and Handheld Technologies* (published by Routledge).

Heather Green is a Senior Lecturer in primary education, specialising in special educational needs and disability at the University of Chichester. Heather also teaches a range of undergraduate and postgraduate courses. Prior to joining the university, she was Assistant Headteacher, and leader and manager of a Resourced Provision for MLD (Moderate Learning Difficulties) at a junior school in Hampshire. Her research interests include inclusive practice and the creative arts, and effective assessment in higher education.

Claire Guthrie, formerly a primary school teacher, is now a Senior Lecturer in Learning Support at City of Glasgow College. In recent years, she has developed an interest in Assistive Technology and Technology Enhanced Learning. Claire currently leads the Assistive Technology Network, a national forum established for professionals supporting students in Further and Higher Education.

Rebecca Heaton is a Senior Lecturer in Education at the University of Northampton. She is curriculum leader for art and design in the Initial Teacher Education division and teaches at undergraduate and postgraduate level. She earned her BAEd with QTS from the University of Reading, MA from Oxford Brookes University, PGCTHE from her home institution and is a HEA Fellow. Prior to working in Higher Education, she taught as Head of Arts and generalist primary practitioner. Her research interests include art education, qualitative research, interdisciplinary practice and digital technology.

Richard Hirstwood is the Director and principal tutor of Hirstwood Training. He is passionate about enabling educators and practitioners to maximise the impact of delivering sensory learning opportunities, in a sensory room or other learning environment, with the resources available to them. His extensive experience is based on practical knowledge, giving him insight into what works and what doesn't in multisensory practice. Regular sessions with children and adults with autism and additional needs, in a variety of multisensory rooms, enable him to maintain this level of excellent practice.

Kara Lawson studied Special Educational Needs and Inclusion at the University of Northampton. Alongside studying, Kara has also worked in the field of autism for the past two years.

Sally Paveley is an experienced teacher and trainer who has a passion for the power of computer-based technologies to transform learning for pupils who have severe and complex special needs. She has been an active participant in the development of ideas and resources in this arena for many years. Sally works at The Bridge School in London where she teaches Computing to secondary aged students who have severe learning difficulties, many of whom are also on the autistic spectrum. She also supports other staff, pupils and parents to develop the use of computer-based technologies throughout the school and beyond though The Bridge Training and Consultancy Service.

Jenni Smith has taught at the Redway School in Milton Keynes for eleven years. She teaches children with SLD and PMLD, and specialises in the teaching of music and communication, ICT and science. She has used a range of ICT equipment in her teaching of music, both in group work and with individual students.

Neil Smith is a Senior Lecturer at the School of Computing and Communications at The Open University. He has taught Computing at a variety of levels, including a range of outreach work in primary and secondary schools and elsewhere. He runs a weekly Code Club, an after-school club for developing programming expertise for primary school children. He has provided CPD and expertise in several contexts, helping teachers and other educators to use Computing and ICT effectively.

Emma Whewell is Curriculum Leader for Physical Education at the University of Northampton, teaching on a number of undergraduate and postgraduate initial teacher training and Sport courses. Prior to this, she taught Physical Education in various secondary schools in Leeds, Bradford and Newcastle as Head of Girls Physical Education and Head of Year. She has a keen interest in technology outdoors and is part of a three-year Erasmus+ project entitled Digital Learning Across Boundaries. Her PhD research is based on newly qualified teachers' understanding of their ideal identity.

Deborah Wilkinson is a Senior Lecturer in primary education, specialising in Science at the University of Chichester. She has 18 years of educational experience working in both schools and initial teacher training.

Karen Woolley is Senior Lecturer and Year 2 Leader at the University of Northampton, specialising in Physical Education, and teaching on a number of undergraduate and postgraduate initial teacher training and Sport courses. Prior to this, she was Head of PE at schools in Cambridge and Northampton. She is keen to share her knowledge of inclusion for all in sport and PE, and to inspire others to engage in a lifelong love for sport. Karen is part of a three-year Erasmus+ project entitled Digital Learning Across Boundaries. Her MA research was based on SEND and pastoral support.

ACKNOWLEDGEMENT

We would like to acknowledge the contribution from Crick Software, which produces award-winning reading and writing software for children of all ages and abilities, including English language learners and those with special educational needs. In addition to Clicker, the company's flagship literacy support tool, Crick's product range includes DocsPlus, a talking word processor for secondary school students, and an exciting range of Clicker apps for iPad and Chromebook.

FOREWORD

Technology can change lives – that's what I like about it. It's not about how many gigabytes are in the box, what the clock speed is, or the name of the processor, but its capacity to change what we do, in part for ourselves, but most significantly for the children and young people we work with.

Take Louisa, a Year 3 child who loved reading but hated writing because her hypermobility meant that holding a pencil quickly became painful. At first, she would write a few lines but later she became very resistant to even starting to put anything on paper as she knew that not only would it hurt, but she wouldn't be able to complete the task. What was the point of even trying? She began to get a reputation for being 'difficult'.

Then the school gave her a Chromebook with a built-in touchscreen – a relatively cheap piece of equipment. Now, not only could she type her work but, if that became bothersome, she could dictate to the machine. Very quickly she became happier, more productive and confidently independent in the classroom.

My indifference towards technology is, I suspect, shared by most adults in the classroom. It may be paradoxical, then, that they are often 'early adopters' of whatever the latest innovation is, mainly because they are constantly on the look-out for ways to connect learners with learning – to give them the opportunities, the experiences and the skills to develop their abilities, and succeed at school and in life, as best as they can.

That early adoption saw much of what we take for granted in our own devices today first emerging in the Special Educational Needs and Disabilities (SEND) field. The speech to text, text to speech, touch screens and voice control we enjoy on our mobile phones and many other gadgets was once specialist and costly, frequently requiring extensive assessments, explicit funding, and specialist support and training to get into the hands of those who needed it. Now these tools are ubiquitous, benefiting learners with the whole gamut of learning difficulties, and none.

Eyegaze is the next technology that will become mainstream. While it started life as a tool for market research, observing where consumers look in shop windows and supermarket aisles, it was quickly recognised as a means of computer access for those with limited mobility. Soon it will be standard in games consoles and, along with voice control, will replace our television remote controls.

While it is a bugbear that technology is too often seen as a panacea for all learning needs, with 'Give him – or her – an iPad' heard much too often, without any consideration of why, it is true that sometimes giving a child a device can make a big difference to them, both for learning and communication, as with Louisa. This is where technology can be life-changing, literally giving a voice to those without one, or putting tools in pupils' hands for them to take control, or to understand and to express themselves in ways that would be impossible without them. It helps to provide independence, access, choice, communication and increasing degrees of autonomy to learners with all and any challenges to learning.

At another level, technology gives us insights into our pupils that would otherwise be unavailable. Eyegaze, for instance, can help us ascertain what is important to learners with little means of communication, what they find interesting, what they want to learn and what they are capable of, through the analytics available to track their gaze, what they look at and for how long.

Technology is also providing us – the adults, the practitioners – with additional powerful tools for teaching, ones that can engage, stimulate, excite, enrich, assess, connect and generally enhance what we do in ways that would not be possible without them. Virtual reality, for instance, can place anyone in a realistic, three-dimensional environment, taking us to places as diverse, perhaps, as a space station, the ocean bed, inside human blood vessels, on a Formula One racetrack, in dire jeopardy on a cliff-edge, or tranquil seclusion on a white sanded beach, simply with a headset, some earphones and a mobile phone. We can practise skills, rehearse responses and experience emotional reactions in safe and secure environments, taking risks and making choices where they can be managed and supported.

The possibilities that technology offers are embraced by SEND teachers, whether in making a multisensory environment with a portable projector, an iPad and a white umbrella, collaborative writing through blogging, immersing learners in out-of-the-ordinary situations with green-screen videos, or simply creating presentations with images, symbols and sound. Technology feeds the creativity of classroom staff, a creativity that underpins much of their practice. It now makes possible tasks that were once the domain of highly trained individuals, such as video making, composing music and producing high-quality printed resources, often with additional elements to aid accessibility, like symbols or Braille-embossed print-outs.

Technology also supports another part of our practice: sharing, which is integral to teaching in developing knowledge, skills and understanding in our learners.

We also use it to share information, whether that's a detailed report from one professional to another, or a photo sent to a parent to celebrate a particular goal being reached. And we share with each other, within classrooms and schools, as well as across our profession. We pass on ideas and information because teaching is essentially a collaborative, collegiate and ultimately giving activity, one where we are always looking for different approaches and know that often the best source of ideas is our fellow practitioners. Once we have them, they get adapted for different pupils in different classrooms and become our own, ready to be passed on again.

Essentially, this book is part of that process. There are numerous good ideas here, taken from working with children and young people with a range of SEND in many different classrooms, which you can take, adapt, build on and make your own, thus generating more good ideas, because education always needs and is never short of fresh ideas.

There are trends in technology that will feed into that process, and we could argue that there are trends in SEND. Then there are the changing demands of the curriculum, assessment and accountability, perhaps following political trends. However, what remains consistent is the creativity, generosity and commitment of teachers in not only meeting the challenges that arise, but also in striving for the best outcomes for the children and young people we work with.

John Galloway
August 2017

INTRODUCTION

Background

Technology has a powerful role to play in supporting the learning and social needs of children with a range of physical, sensory, communication or cognitive disabilities. For many such children technology means that they can be included in lessons and access a wider curriculum; for some, it is the only way for them to make their thoughts and needs known. According to the Department for Education (2015), 15.4 per cent of pupils in England have identified special educational needs or disabilities (SEND). This equates to well over a million pupils (Department of Education, 2015). There are many different levels of SEND, and it has been estimated that as many as 1 in 5 children may need extra learning support at some stage (see: www.ttrb3.org.uk/audit-commission-special-educational-needs-a-mainstream-issue). Research evidence suggests that technology can support inclusion by enabling greater autonomy, assisting with communication and promoting practices that reach beyond the school (Becta, 2003). In the light of this data, we are delighted to have been able to collect experiences and ideas from a wide range of education specialists in this practice guide.

In recent years, there has been increased convergence between specialist *assistive technology*, which helps people with SEND to overcome the additional challenges they face in communication and learning, and the broader field of *educational technology*, which can benefit all students. Both fields have been marked by rapid change, and the implementation of technologies in the classroom can, at times, be demanding and daunting for teachers.

Recently, we have seen an uptake of mobile devices accompanied by the phasing out of computer suites; new devices are emerging based on eyegaze, augmented and virtual reality, gesture and thought control; there is an increase in technology-enabled multisensory environments, in the use of robots and drones for telepresence, and in the use of music and media technologies for digital creativity. Developments such as these offer many possibilities for extending the range of experiential learning for pupils with SEND. As a result, technology for inclusion is evolving fast and is presenting new challenges to teachers. At the same time, local authority support is dwindling and there are fewer specialist advisory teachers supporting individuals or providing teacher CPD. If they are to maximise the impact of technology, teachers and support staff need to fully understand its potential and learn how to tailor its use to suit individual needs.

Overview

By drawing on examples from current classroom practice, this book provides an up-to-date guide to how educational and assistive technologies can be used in combination to embed inclusive approaches across the primary subjects. Our examples take the form of mini case studies, aiming for a balance across types of technologies, special and mainstream contexts, pupil ages and the range of SEND. We aim to show how technologies can be used in inclusive whole-class teaching, as well as illustrating how they can be tailored to improve access to the curriculum for individuals.

There is a focus on cutting-edge technologies that promote engagement, and support collaborative and active learning across curriculum subjects so that they are embedded as creative tools. We also look at how technologies can provide a rich and accessible learning environment for pupils with SEND, and how they can be sensitively combined to produce personalised learning solutions.

Following on from the case studies, chapter discussion sections reflect on aspects of pedagogy, such as how best to differentiate across a range of abilities and needs, assessment *for* learning and *of* learning in the context of SEND, the teacher's role and pupil progression. These discussions are supported by relevant theory and research evidence. The aim is to offer a framework of strategies for integrating technology into existing learning contexts in meaningful ways.

The chapters

Each chapter is based on a curriculum theme and gives consideration as to how technology can address each of the four broad areas of need identified in the SEN Code of Practice (Department for Education, 2014) by helping learners collaborate, be in control, create and access digital content. The four areas of need are 'communication and interaction', 'cognition and learning', 'social, emotional and mental health', and 'sensory and/or physical needs'.

Chapter 1 explores the theme of multisensory storytelling: how technology can be used to develop narratives and make stories available to an audience whose communication needs are different. Carefully chosen pieces of technology enable us to use all our senses to bring an extra dimension to a story, reinforcing its concepts and creating impact and drama. This makes engagement irresistible. An example combines a virtual roller coaster ride using the 'Coaster Physics' app, a Pico projector and a white pop-up tent. The authors recognise that limitations of movement, vision, hearing, cognition, behaviour and perception inhibit children's enjoyment of life, and they suggest that multisensory environments can provide opportunities for bridging some of these barriers. Within immersive storytelling environments, children can move between digital and physical spaces to explore narrative using low- and high-tech resources. Combining tactile materials with sound, projected images and light, gives them a space in which to collaborate and be in control.

Chapter 2 is based on technology supporting literacy. It suggests that reducing the emphasis on text-heavy lessons can help break down reading and writing barriers. There are examples of visual strategies, such as symbol-based software, colour-coded sentences, and images supporting reading and writing. This chapter also shows how the use of sound through talking word processors, eBooks or narration options can enable children to engage more deeply with text. Universal Design for Learning (UDL) is an approach that creates flexible learning environments accommodating individual differences through multiple means of representation, expression and engagement.

The theme of Chapter 3 is outdoor learning. There is an emphasis on using technologies such as iPads and tablets, GPS trackers, GoPro cameras, nature identification apps and drones to engage with the physical world. Such devices offer the potential to look at the world through a different lens and can provide new avenues for children to interact with their surroundings. Examples include creating trails, safaris and treasure hunts based on images and sounds using mobile devices. These provide an open-ended and flexible way for children to explore the outdoors and then share their experiences with others. Creating digital artefacts together to document outdoor journeys is a way of engaging children to take ownership of the direction of their learning and to develop social skills alongside. Playful use of technology outdoors can also foster positive transitions to new environments.

Chapter 4 demonstrates how accessible musical instruments such as the Soundbeam or Skoog can enhance musicianship and communication for children with severe or profound and multiple learning difficulties. The medium of sound can promote interaction and communication as well as stimulate musical appreciation. It can also be integrated with other curriculum activities as a cue, as an expressive tool or to introduce learning themes or stories. The 'Sounds of Intent' assessment framework is shared as a tool for documenting the learning progression of children with SENDs in music.

Chapter 5 considers how technology can support children as scientific researchers and inquirers. The case studies focus on creating accessible practical science activities within meaningful contexts, such as stories or real-world events to stimulate curiosity. They suggest using a range of tools including iPads, QR codes and video both during and after the science data collection process to support observational skills, the presentation of findings and the interpretation of data.

Chapter 6 also focuses on practical activities, this time within the curriculum area of Design and Technology. Lego WeDo, Makey Makey, Raspberry Pis and Micro:bits are suggested as tools that allow children to reach goals through trial and error, a key aspect of computational thinking. Once again, the need to provide a context which engages learners is recognised. One case study is based on creating a new toy for a Dragons' Den-style challenge and a second uses an online music tool to explore sounds of a rainforest accompanied by sensory experiences. Ideas for developing food technology themes with SEND pupils are also explored.

Our computing chapter (Chapter 7) begins with a wonderful example of a reluctant learner becoming highly engaged with programming in his very own Raspberry Pi workshop. Next, the authors find a new use for symbols as a tool for creating visual algorithms for kinaesthetic and 'unplugged' robot games. There are many practical examples of applying computational thinking across the curriculum. For example, making links between coding and dance can help to build metacognition around computational thinking so that the strategies are explicit and transferable. Using the language of computational thinking in everyday tasks demystifies it for children. By approaching computer science as a broad and creative subject to be explored both on- and off-screen through everyday tasks, rather than as a narrow discipline, we can meet a diverse range of learning needs.

Chapter 8 presents ideas for using technology for inclusive creative arts. These include interconnected physical and digital creative arts experiences and interdisciplinary approaches. One way of promoting inclusion is to produce collaborative images, and photo manipulation tools are suggested as a way of working together to make photo collages. In a second example, greenscreening is used to exchange 'virtual sculptures' and place them in different locations. In this way, art becomes a tool for connecting classrooms, and a context for social learning and communication. Conceptual art is another approach that can help to develop empathy. Gesture-based technologies such as Leap Motion or Kinect, in conjunction with sensory apps such as Visikord or ReacTickles, can enable pupils with limited mobility to turn sound or movements into expressive and visually captivating outputs.

The theme of our final chapter is Personal, Social and Emotional Development, or PSED. A range of technologies are suggested for supporting life skills, for games-based learning and leisure, for creating social stories, for independent living skills, and for helping children understand health, safety and risk. The case studies illustrate how augmented and virtual reality can energise and enthuse learners. Virtual field trips can provide opportunities to learn about difference, equality and rights. The Somantics suite based on touch and gesture is suggested to offer disengaged children the opportunity to interact with visual displays through movement.

Creating a supportive classroom

A key theme across all chapters is describing what a supportive and inclusive classroom looks like in practice. Many of our contributors note that the assessment of needs and the finding of technology-based learning solutions is very much an individualised process. However, there are some universally useful software tools aimed at SEND learners, and they acknowledge the importance of exploring customisation options and personalised learning approaches within these. Our mobile and desktop devices and browser plugins have built-in accessibility options such as magnification, colours and contrast choices, page decluttering, sound recording, text to speech and voice recognition. Many of these can make reading and writing more comfortable and efficient for our learners.

Alongside these options, there is a plethora of free or low-cost apps and tools available for teaching specific skills, for content creation and for increasing productivity. Perhaps the most useful of these are the open-ended apps that can be used repeatedly: apps for making eBooks, for editing video, for making interactive images or for creating talking screencasts, to give a few examples.

We could argue that the most significant contribution made by technology, then, is choice: it can offer a variety of visual and auditory access methods, and a range of ways of handling print and recording ideas. These give children options for accessing content and a chance to present their learning outcomes using a range of media. Separating the mechanics of writing can help children to keep better pace with the flow of their ideas, making the learning process more satisfying.

To summarise, some key learning strategies for supporting children with SEND include:

- promoting independence through customised routines, and individual and differentiated choices;

- using eBook formats with screen adjustments, sound, highlighted text and voice recording for active reading and responding;

- flipped learning approaches allowing choice over ways into topics, and control over the pace and place of learning;

- Bring Your Own Devices (BYOD) to personalise learning through purposeful media-rich approaches;

- collaborative ways of working using tools such as Google Apps for Education and Office 365;

- supporting access to print with visuals, sound and media.

Another exciting theme across the book chapters is the use of technology to enable children to do things that they would never be able to do otherwise. Emerging technologies offer exciting new conduits for learning. Examples include the use of drones or robots for telepresence (that is, the ability to be elsewhere through virtual means), the use of augmented reality supporting hearing-impaired learners by adding subtitles to faces in real time, or the addition of a reading device to a pair of glasses to quickly identify objects and faces or read text aloud. Lifelike robots are being used as a social mediator for children with autism. Virtual reality field trips have huge potential to engage children by immersing them in places that they have never seen in real life. They can also offer a safe practice environment for trying out social skills.

Eyegaze and gesture-based technologies allow learners with poor physical mobility to interact meaningfully and independently with the digital world, and can also be a communication tool for pupils with limited speech. Conversely, eyegaze tracking can become a window into the minds of children as we can analyse their visual field. Technology is even being used for mind control using headsets that respond to brain activity. The most crucial aspect of these innovations is that the technology enables children to do more things for themselves.

At the same time, technology does not have to be cutting-edge to make an impact. Sometimes it is the simple apps and tools that make the biggest difference. Our contributors draw attention to tools and apps that promote independent living, enabling children to become more confident in managing day-to-day tasks: talking clocks, money readers, talking tins and labels, recogniser apps, liquid level indicators, and money-recognition devices, to name a few.

In conclusion, we acknowledge the need to embed the use of technology in SEND contexts through immersive approaches that mix physical and digital learning spaces. Rather than sitting children in front of computer screens, we aim to integrate creative uses of technology into real-world engagement. We look to take devices out and about with us, and create socially and sensory-rich experiential learning opportunities across the curriculum. As a result, we can tap into children's confidence with technology to address their learning challenges and enable them to explore and build new meanings through collaboration and control.

Helen Caldwell

References

Becta (2003). *What the research says about ICT supporting special educational needs (SEN) and inclusion.* British Educational Communications and Technology Agency (BECTA). Coventry.

Department for Education (2014). *Special educational needs and disability code of practice: 0 to 25 years.* Crown.

Department for Education (2015). *Statistical First Release: Special educational needs in England.* Crown.

Chapter 1

MULTISENSORY STORYTELLING

RICHARD HIRSTWOOD

Introduction

Story-telling is an age-old tradition across human cultures worldwide. The spoken story began it all, retelling significant events, most likely supported with the tales being acted out. This was followed by a drawn version, typified by cave paintings. Sensory stories are therefore nothing new. What is new is the application of the fantastic technologies available to us now.

This chapter, then, will explore how technology is being used to develop narratives and, more especially, make these stories available to an audience whose communication needs are different, whether these differences stem from sensory losses such as vision, hearing or movement, or to those whose cognitive differences mean they require as much support as is available, and to those individuals who need more time and more repetition to grasp the concepts expressed. Indeed, everyone can enjoy and benefit from the impact that technology can bring to sensory stories.

First, what sensory stories are and why they are of benefit to learners with special educational needs and disabilities (SEND) will be briefly considered. The relevance of sensory stories and learning styles will then be explored. How sensory stories can be an even more effective teaching tool when reinforced with the appropriate and relevant use of technology matched to a learner's learning styles will be highlighted. Which environments are most suited to the delivery of sensory stories and why will also be discussed. Throughout this chapter, using case studies, different ways of using sensory stories reinforced by technology with pupils with SEND will be suggested.

Learning objectives

By the end of this chapter you should be able to:

- differentiate a sensory story appropriately, using a wide range of strategies that enable pupils to be taught effectively;
- create a stimulating learning environment to capture pupils' imagination and engagement in a sensory story;
- understand how technology can reduce/inhibit factors that may cause a barrier to pupils learning and participation in a sensory story;
- match an individual's learning styles to appropriate technology.

Links to Teachers' Standards

1. **Set high expectations which inspire, motivate and challenge pupils**

   - establish a safe and stimulating environment for pupils, rooted in mutual respect;
   - set goals that stretch and challenge pupils of all backgrounds, abilities and dispositions.

2. **Promote good progress and outcomes by pupils**

   - be accountable for pupils' attainment, progress and outcomes;
   - be aware of pupils' capabilities and their prior knowledge, and plan teaching to build on these;
   - guide pupils to reflect on the progress they have made and their emerging needs;
   - demonstrate knowledge and understanding of how pupils learn and how this impacts on teaching;
   - encourage pupils to take a responsible and conscientious attitude to their own work and study.

5. **Adapt teaching to respond to the strengths and needs of all pupils**

   - know when and how to differentiate appropriately, using approaches which enable pupils to be taught effectively;
   - have a secure understanding of how a range of factors can inhibit pupils' ability to learn, and how best to overcome these;
   - demonstrate an awareness of the physical, social and intellectual development of children, and know how to adapt teaching to support pupils' education at different stages of development;
   - have a clear understanding of the needs of all pupils, including those with special educational needs; those of high ability; those with English as an additional language; those with disabilities; and be able to use and evaluate distinctive teaching approaches to engage and support them.

6. **Make accurate and productive use of assessment**

   - give pupils regular feedback, both orally and through accurate marking, and encourage pupils to respond to the feedback.

Links to National SENCO Standards

National SENCO Standards (DfE, 2015)

9. **Develop, implement, monitor and evaluate systems to:**
    Record and review the progress of children and young people with SEN and/or disabilities;

4. **Strategies for improving outcomes for pupils with SEN and/or disabilities**
    The potential of new technologies to support communication, teaching and learning for children and young people with SEN and/or disabilities.

Part C: Personal and Professional Qualities
There are high expectations for all children and young people with SEN and/or disabilities.

Person-centred approaches build upon and extend the experiences, interests, skills and knowledge of children and young people with SEN and/or disabilities.

Links to National Curriculum Programmes of Study (DfE, 2013)

English: Children use discussion in order to learn; they should be able to elaborate and explain clearly their understanding and ideas.

Computing: Children are responsible, competent, confident and creative users of information and communication technology.

Case study 1: Sensory stories in the classroom

Fountaindale School deliver their curriculum through play. This approach relies very much on the inventiveness of the practitioner to create sensory learning opportunities which use appropriate mobile technology to reinforce learning. The use of sensory stories as a teaching tool is embedded in everyday classroom activities.

A class of nine semi-formal learners, all wheelchair users with varied levels of cognitive abilities, are taking part in a lesson about volcanoes. All learn better with enhanced multisensory stimulation, with a strong focus on developing communication skills.

Their learning is delivered through the vehicle of an individual and specifically scripted sensory story, which takes place every Monday at 11am and is repeated weekly, in an expanding series of events, building upon the story week by week. It is designed to revisit areas of the curriculum previously taught and to remind the pupils of concepts they have experienced in previous lessons. An interactive learning wall illustrates the concepts taught and provides a focus for pupils to engage with.

The story develops over the term, expanding in length and complexity as the pupils learn more concepts. The script of the sensory story is set and the sequence does not vary, which enables the pupils to get to know each part of the story and to begin to predict the next part of the sequence. New concepts are introduced within this familiar context.

What are the key features of this approach?

- The sensory story is unique to the specific curriculum elements the class are learning.

- The story is multisensory and is appropriate to meet the varied learning styles of the pupils.

- The sensory story is carefully scripted and follows the same sequence, adding new concepts within this routine.

- The sensory story is represented in the classroom by a multisensory 'learning wall'.

- Repetition of key concepts within a familiar learning routine reinforces learning for pupils over a greater number of learning opportunities.

- The sensory story is also referred to throughout the week's lessons and specific parts are revisited on a day-to-day basis.

But how is technology used in the classroom for these curriculum sensory stories?

Gathering around the teacher and the learning wall, the pupils experience the sensory story which is told by the teacher, supported by a team of skilled classroom assistants. The technology used in the sensory story is prepared and within reach before the story begins. Relatively simple technology, such as a microphone to give the pupils a voice, is very effective and creates an enthusiasm in the pupils to participate: 'who wants to shout it out?'

The key feature of the technology used here is that it is not being used just for the sake of using technology. It is used to enhance the story and reinforce its concepts. It is used to create impact and drama – to be irresistible for pupils to engage with learning.

It does not feel as if it should not be there. Each carefully chosen piece of technology brings an extra dimension or a reinforcing tool not available to the teacher in any other way.

It does not play a central role. If the technology fails, it is not a problem because it is a part of the story, not the key tool or delivery system.

Care is taken to make sure that this is a multisensory story, not just a sound and lighting experience. So, in addition to the visual and sound technological effects, specific experiences have been identified, created and are offered to enhance the pupils' tactile, gustatory, olfactory, vestibular and proprioceptive sensory skills.

Fountaindale School uses sensory stories as a vehicle for increasing the number of opportunities for pupils to revisit their learning, by the use of repetition of key concepts within a familiar learning routine. The technology used is not the key focus of the story; it is used to reinforce concepts and embed the learning. The technology used is simple and really effective. And, because the technology is kept simple, it works.

Reflective questions

- Should you adapt books as sensory stories or make them up yourself?

- What will be the result of your intervention with a sensory story?

- How will this shape what and how you deliver your sensory story?

- What technology should be chosen to enhance the pupils' learning experience, and why?

Case study 2: Solitary or shared stories?

We often think of a sensory story as being a shared experience – one that promotes interaction, communication and engagement between peers. Supporting technology builds on these core skills. But when can a solitary sensory story with very simple technology be of great benefit?

A teenage boy with autism is finding the traditional classroom teaching situation too demanding. Too many different and changing activities in the classroom mean that he exhibits behaviours that staff find challenging to manage and which result in very limited engagement with any presented activities – lasting brief seconds, if at all.

It is decided to take the session into the sensory room, as this environment offers:

- a controllable space;

- reduced visual and sound clutter;

- fewer people to reduce distraction;

- one-to-one attention.

Using one simple stimulus in the sensory room enables the young man to focus on this, rather than having to cope with several different stimuli occurring around the classroom, which is too bombarding.

A simple, repetitive sensory story develops a familiarity to make him at ease in his new environment. Sitting next to the bubble tube, the story 'Many Coloured Days' begins. Coloured switches switch the bubble tube on and off, and control the colours of the bubbles to match those in the story.

No demands to look, listen or be near are made: the calm environment, the bubbles and the storytelling are the attraction for the young man to engage with. The first page is read, then the second. These are repeated, while the bubble tube changes colour, matching the colours in the story. During these first few pages of the story, the young man paces around the room. After repeating these pages several times more, his interest is aroused and he comes over and joins the storyteller. Still no demands are made. After repeating the same two pages several times more, spontaneously he presses himself up against the bubble tube and listens. This interaction is on his terms once he becomes familiar with the routine of the story and the colour changing bubbles. He engages for a minute before moving away to the other side of the sensory room. After a few moments, he returns to the bubble tube and the story starts again. This happens four or five times before he really begins to engage and interact. He shows pleasure and enjoyment with the shared sensory story, focusing on the storyteller, the bubbles and the story for the next 20 minutes.

Could the session have been developed without the bubble tube? The answer, in this case, is no. The young man needed the experience to be multisensory to be engaging. The technology was used to attract his attention and draw him into the session. His interest was initially in the colour-changing bubbles but, as he became more relaxed and familiar with events, he began to explore more of the aspects of the experience available to him. This creates further opportunities for him to engage – e.g. to control the bubble tube using the switch, as he becomes more and more interested in a broader range of experiences within the sensory space.

For this young man, a solitary sensory story with one multisensory stimulus for focus enabled him to successfully engage with a learning experience.

Reflective questions

- How can we identify when a shared or solitary sensory story is most appropriate?

- By which means can we assess which elements of an environment provide too much or too little stimulation?

Case study 3: Sensory stories, iPad apps and 'on-looker' engagement

Occasionally, the beneficiary of the sensory story is not who you had intended. Using iPad apps and projection can create a reason to interact too strong to refuse, even for pupils described as 'in their own world' or 'difficult to reach'.

A small group of mixed-ability learners are taking a 'virtual' roller-coaster ride using the Coaster Physics app, a pico projector and a white pop-up tent. The story of taking the roller-coaster ride is the vehicle for introducing and practising various mathematical concepts of up/down, fast/slow, etc.

One pupil with autism sits away from the group, using 'in ear' headphones to reduce sound 'clutter' and shows little engagement with any aspect of his environment. He finds it difficult to tolerate other people and avoids eye contact.

The group taking the virtual roller-coaster ride are shouting and screaming as they dip and turn, and the initial aim of the session, for the pupil to join the roller-coaster activity, is revised. His 'in ear' headphones reduce the groups' noise, but the large-scale projected image of the roller-coaster remains in his sight.

After several trips around the track, the pupil begins to show a fleeting interest in the visual imagery of the roller-coaster. Maintaining his distance, his gaze is increasingly upon the tent and his level of attention increases.

The group moves on to another activity to explore the mathematical concepts experienced on the roller-coaster. The projected image of the coaster remains on the tent. With a clear space, the boy comes nearer to the tent and the image. The roller-coaster begins with the boy very close to the visual image.

The boy is now very engaged with the roller-coaster experience, secure in the tent environment which is small and which reduces other visual clutter in the space. A classroom assistant moves into the tent, sharing the experience of taking the roller-coaster ride with him. Non-verbal communication strategies reduce the potential bombardment of extra information, which may overload the boy.

For this young boy with autism, who initially could not tolerate a shared activity and was isolated from the group, time and technology proved too engaging for him to ignore. His initial engagement was through technology, but exploration of the story and experiencing the roller-coaster in isolation eventually led to a shared activity and interaction with another individual.

Reflective questions

- How can we use our knowledge of pupils' sensory skills to identify and record progress towards appropriate targets?

- What strategies can you use to make the learning experience irresistible for your pupils to engage with?

What is a sensory story?

A sensory story is one that is brought to life by presenting the narrative using powerful multisensory experiences. In other words, highlighting the visual, auditory, tactile, gustatory, olfactory, vestibular and proprioceptive aspects of the story. Presented in this manner, a sensory story will have greater meaning to a learner who has a sensory loss or multisensory impairment. A strong, but simple story narrative reinforces these sensory elements.

Sensory stories and learning styles

Learning styles, as described by Howard Gardner (1983), support the idea of delivering stories in a multisensory fashion, to ensure the inclusion of learners with a variety of learning styles. As learners may have a combination of different learning styles, a sensory story ensures that learning is delivered via multiple accessible channels rather than a single one, which may or may not be accessible for that specific learner at that specific time. Later, we will explore in more detail the relevance of learning styles to sensory stories, matched with appropriate technology.

Who benefits from a sensory story?

For all learners, with or without SEND, sensory stories can be much more meaningful than stories read in the traditional manner. A learner with a hearing impairment is given the opportunity to experience the story using their stronger/other sensory skills – i.e. 'feeling' and 'seeing' the story, rather than experiencing the story only via their impaired sensory skill – their hearing. Multisensory presentation of a story 'scaffolds' weaker/impaired sensory skills using a learner's more dominant/stronger sensory skills. For learners with autism, a sensory story can have the predictability required to help them become familiar with a specific learning experience or routine. Repetition and familiarity reduce anxiety and confusion, enabling the learner with autism to engage more easily in their learning. However, sensory stories are also of benefit to individuals with communication impairments, social, emotional and mental health issues, and dementia – not just learners with complex learning needs.

Sensory stories and repetition, repetition, repetition

One of the strengths of a sensory story is that it is often repeated many times over, as indeed it should be. We saw from the case study of Fountaindale School how they use repetition to strengthen learning for their pupils. Preece and Zhao's (2015) sensory storytelling strategy noted the importance of consistency and structure. The learning experience becomes embedded and meaningful, helping a learner to develop communication skills, as well as other skills such as prediction and concept formation.

Neuroscience also supports this premise. The brain needs to practise to develop. In brief, the cells in the brain communicate via chemicals linking cells to cells. When this process is repeated many times, the chemical, or message, becomes more adept at travelling between the two neurons. Repetition of this process embeds the skill to the point where it becomes easier and, sometimes, almost automatic. This is summed up by the phrase *Cells that fire together, wire together* (Hebbian theory) outlined by Siegrid Löwel (1949).

When is technology appropriate for a sensory story?

Technology should enhance a sensory story, empower learners to engage with the experience and bring an extra dimension not possible in another way. It should be used so that the learners have access to a broader, more appropriate, method of story delivery.

Our technological toolkit should be appropriate and empowering. So, use an iPad because the content is more engaging for a visual learner; use a bubble tube because the learner can feel the experience as well as see it; or use a switch to enable the learner to make a meaningful contribution, or to take a turn, in the sequence of the story.

Technology is not appropriate for a sensory story when its impact/effect is not understood by the practitioner; when the practitioner is unfamiliar with how to operate it; when it is not relevant or its meaning within the story has not been fully considered; when it is not accessible to the learners or its justification in the story toolkit is because it is 'new'.

Differentiation of the sensory story

Technology can really enhance a sensory story by delivering strong sensory stimuli. However, different learners access the sensory information in the sensory story at different levels, irrespective of how it is presented to them. These levels are described below.

Level one: experiential learners
Learners begin to show an awareness to sensory input. These sensory experiences reinforce the brain's response to an action or a 'unique event' (as described by Norman Doidge), developing a recognition of consistently presented sensory experiences.

At this level of interaction, the learner will experience:

- vision: light/dark/colour/form/shape;

- hearing: frequency, soft/loud, fast/slow, stationary, directional, motion;

- touch: soft/hard/smooth/rough/stationary/motion;

- taste: bitter/sweet/salt/sour/related;

- smell: pleasant/unpleasant/related.

Level two: understanding elements
A learner may experience and understand key elements or concepts of the theme or session in isolation, but not generalise it to other related concepts/themes.

Level three: fully engaged with learning
Learners working at this level understand the sequence of the story, and the concepts and outcomes contained within it.

Matching technology to learning styles in a sensory story

The work of such people as Howard Gardner (1983) and Barbara Prashnig (1998) has raised the profile of individual learning styles or, as Clive Smith describes them, 'learning strengths' (Hirstwood and Smith, 2012).

Yet, there is little reference to the concept of individual learning styles in the education of pupils with SEND. Where reference is made, it all almost universally focuses upon the visual learning style, as promoted by and reinforced by the work of Temple Grandin (1995) in *Thinking in Pictures*.

So, does the concept of learning styles have any further positive contribution to make to our teaching style when working with learners with SEND?

Much of the technology employed in sensory stories is visual and practitioners need to ensure that technology is also employed to support the development of the other senses. We need to create and deliver sensory stories that meet an individual's multiple learning styles, utilising the most appropriate technology available to us.

However, a word of caution. While it is useful to offer multiple ways of accessing learning, it may not be as useful to identify an individual as only a particular type of learner – i.e. only a visual learner etc. Hood *et al.* (2017) offer a different viewpoint on evidence supporting the existence of learning styles.

Below, we look at the various learning styles, as described by Howard Gardner, and offer suggestions as to how technology can be matched to these and incorporated into an individual's learning experiences during a sensory story.

Portable technology

iPads, android devices and portable laptops are wonderful tools and are increasingly available to use within your sensory story. In a digital world where content is king, a good internet connection and an account with Apple's App Store or the Android Play Store will mean that you have access to a massive number of apps, covering some subjects you know and those you may never have heard of. However, beware. Steve Jobs famously said: 'There's an app for that', a phrase that is now trademarked by Apple, and he was right. Too many apps are not necessarily a good thing.

Evaluate each app in terms of its value and effectiveness for its role in the story.

- Is it relevant?

- Is it motivating?

- What skills will it target?

- Can you individualise the content?

- What feedback will it give to the learner?

Think of an app as a tool. What will it enable you to do that you cannot do now? Can you break down the app into manageable parts so you do not overwhelm the learner with too much information?

'Epic Citadel', mentioned later in this chapter, is the backdrop for Infinity Blade. A medieval kingdom, it provides the ability for the learner to explore each part of the citadel. It is not a story as such, but it is a blank canvas for you to create your sensory story against.

Mobile technology also gives the practitioner the ability to connect to a projector, creating a large-scale or small image as required (see Visual Learning Styles for further information about projectors). Additional props, such as tents, umbrellas, mosquito nets and sheets bring the visual imagery to life, while reducing other visual distractions – i.e. glare from the windows.

Immersive rooms and sensory stories

What is an immersive room? A sensory room could be described as an immersive room, as could a tent or a cardboard box. In many schools, immersive rooms are what some people term 'digital environments' or 'visual digital environments'. The term 'immersive room' is used in this context to describe a blank canvas, where all walls can be covered in projected still or moving imagery.

Immersive rooms with interactive hot-spots can give the learners a chance to interact in a way with a story or experience, which is not achievable in a traditional sensory room or other environment. Learners may explore the scenario independently, creating their own contribution to the story. However, some learners may find the increased stimuli the vestibular and proprioceptive systems are exposed to in an immersive environment too unbalancing and unnerving to engage with learning.

As the technology in immersive environments continues to develop, we may find a greater reliability and controllability of these systems, which will be easier for the practitioner to use.

Many bespoke immersive systems seen in schools today lack the content required to meet the needs of an ever-changing group of learners. New content may not be easy to generate for the practitioner, who then relies on pre-loaded content to contribute to the story or scenario.

We must also be mindful that immersive rooms should not just be a digital visual environment for a sensory story. A true sensory story should also focus on and support the learner's other sensory systems.

Sensory stories in multisensory rooms

A multisensory room offers practitioners a controlled space to focus on the development of a learner's visual, auditory, tactile, gustatory, olfactory, vestibular and proprioceptive senses – the whole sensory system. Unlike other spaces, such as a classroom, practitioners have a high degree of control over the sensory stimulus presented. Professor Paul Pagliano (2012) reminds us that a well-designed sensory room is a place where we can *increase or decrease a stimulus and use it in isolation or in combination*. In other words, custom design the space and sensory stimuli for optimal learning for an individual.

The multisensory room is often jam-packed full of technology. Some systems are based on PC software and may be difficult to program and therefore control. Complex control systems often mean that the sensory room may be underused or focus mostly on visual and auditory effects.

Here's where the 'AAA' principles of a multisensory room fit in – availability, appropriateness and achievability. Your multisensory tools and equipment need to be available when you need them and to work first time. Does your multisensory room really suit all the learning styles and needs of the learners who use it? For example, a visually cluttered room certainly will not suit the learning style of those with autism. Does the design of your multisensory room mean that it allows all practitioners to use the equipment without a vast technical knowledge? Simplicity is often the best way forward. Why have lots of complicated equipment (that no one will use) when you can have a few easy to operate and effective multisensory tools that will be in continuous use?

In terms of their sensory system, what can the learner experience in a multisensory room? Here, the potential is only limited by the practitioners' imagination. From the more obvious visual awareness/fixation/tracking to reducing light sensitivity; from auditory discrimination to auditory sequencing; from awareness, responding and initiation to awareness of others; exploring 'self' or turn-taking with another – the learning opportunities are endless. Bozic (1997) comments that *educational technology cannot be evaluated in isolation from the educational practices within which it is situated*. In other words, the technology itself is only as important as the way in which the practitioner uses it.

Each piece of equipment or technology in the sensory space should be regarded as a tool – a means to an end, delivered via the vehicle of a sensory story. How will using a bubble tube enable the learner to develop sound location skills? For learners who need to establish joint attention, how will using small-scale projected images facilitate this?

So, the sensory room provides an ideal environment to combine strong sensory stimuli with the simple narrative of a story. Learners may engage on a variety of levels, from simple experiential to more fully immersive. The multisensory approach offers potential for learners to become involved with the narrative content through a range of sensory routes, resulting in a higher level of interactivity.

Summary and Key Points

This chapter has explored the many ways in which technology has a role to play in sensory storytelling. From specific technology and apps to more 'low-tech' interventions, we have seen how these tools can contribute to the creation of an engaging and irresistible learning experience within a sensory story. We have explored how technology can support or detract from a learning opportunity, which is often dependent on the practitioner's skill in using the specific technology. Never forget, however, that the most engaging, multisensory experience in a learner's world is you.

References

Bozic, N (1997) Constructing the room: Multisensory rooms in educational contexts. *European Journal of Special Needs Education*, 12(1): 54–70.

Department for Education (DfE) (2013) *The National Curriculum in England: Key Stages 1 and 2 Framework*. Available at: www.gov.uk/government/publications/national-curriculum-in-england-primary-curriculum (accessed 6 December 2016).

Department for Education (2015) *SEND Code of Practice: 0–25 years*. Available at: www.gov.uk/government/publications/send-code-of-practice-0-to-25 (accessed 28 July 2017).

Doidge, N (2007) *The Brain that Changes Itself: Stories of Personal Triumph from the Frontiers of Brain Science*. London: Penguin.

Gardner, H (1983) *Frames of Mind: The Theory of Multiple Intelligences*. London: Fontana Press.

Grandin, T (1995) *Thinking in Pictures*. New York: Vintage Books/Random House.

Hirstwood, R and Smith, C (2012) Learning styles and autism. Available at: www.hirstwood.com/course-notes/autism-pages/learning-styles-and-autism (accessed 20 June 2017).

Hood, B *et al*. (2017) No evidence to back idea of learning styles. Available at: www.theguardian.com/education/2017/mar/12/no-evidence-to-back-idea-of-learning-styles (accessed 20 June 2017).

Löwel, S (1949) *The Organization of Behavior*. New York: Wiley & Sons.

Pagliano, P (2012) *The Multisensory Handbook*. London: Routledge.

Prashnig, B (1998) *The Power of Diversity: New Ways of Learning and Teaching through Learning Styles*. Auckland, NZ: David Bateman.

Preece, D and Zhao, Y (2015) Multi-sensory storytelling: A tool for teaching or an intervention. *British Journal of Special Education*, 42(4): 429–43.

Apps and tools for multisensory storytelling

App or tool	What it does	Type
Sound and music		
Roland VT3 Voice Transformer	Change the tone/pitch/frequency of the storyteller's voice Enable learners to contribute a vocalisation to the story Turn a voice into a musical instrument and sing with harmonies	Hardware
Songify by Smule	Automatically turns speech into music.	iOs and Android
CSTR Physics Can be used with: Car Dash by Andy Pidcock	Design and ride your very own realistic roller coaster, and see how variables like speed, acceleration, energy and g-force change as you ride along the track. Car dash is music which stops and starts, providing the learner with the opportunity to start/stop the roller coaster in the CSTR Physics App. https://youtu.be/hS826kzMn5c	iOS YouTube
ThumbJam	An iPad synth which realistically re-creates the sound of many instruments like violins and pianos.	iOS
Bloom by Brian Eno Can be used with: WoWee	Allows you to create elaborate patterns and unique melodies by simply tapping the screen. A portable gel speaker which turns any surface into a subwoofer, emitting strong vibrations making sound accessible for those with a hearing loss. http://www.woweeone.com/	iOS Hardware
Pretorian Applicator Can be used with: Drawing with Stars by L'Escapadou and with: Sensory Sound Box by Cognable	A bluetooth device which acts as a switch interface between a switch and an iOS or Android device. http://www.pretorianuk.com/applicator An app, which can be switch controlled, and allows you to draw with animated stars. This is a developmental touch skills app, with the capacity for switch control. It was made for children with complex learning needs including autism and visual impairment.	Hardware iOS iOS
Sensory Light Box by Cognable	Light Box uses abstract animation and sound to introduce basic touch skills and awareness.	iOS
Little Fox Music Box by Fox and Sheep GmbH	An interactive sing-along book, with the ability to record your own songs.	iOS
Sources of music to accompany your Sensory Story include:	SoundCloud – https://soundcloud.com/ Spotify – https://www.spotify.com/uk/ Amazon Music – https://www.amazon.co.uk/gp/dmusic/promotions/PrimeMusic Apple Music – http://www.apple.com/uk/music/ Andy Pidcock – http://www.andypidcock.com/	Web Tools

App or tool	What it does	Type
Noise cancelling headphones	For some learners, particularly those with autism, noise-cancelling headphones give them the ability to modulate/regulate sensory stimuli around them. A transition from these to bone conduction headphones would maintain the ability to self-modulate whilst developing awareness to background sounds within their environment.	Hardware
Bone conduction headphones	https://aftershokz.co.uk/	Hardware
Kinaesthetic apps		
Xbox Playstation	Gesture controlled technology enables learners to interact with their learning, but is rarely seen in special schools. However, these platforms do offer games and experiences relevant to our learners.	Hardware
Sound Beam	A touch free device which uses sensor technology to translate body movement into music and sound. http://www.soundbeam.co.uk/	Hardware
Omi Vista by OMI	A projection system that responds to gesture and movement, creating dynamic images on any surface. http://omi.uk/omivista-interactive-floor/	Hardware
Magic Carpet by Sensory Guru	A dynamic projection system, creating dynamic imagery. http://www.sensoryguru.com/product/mobile-magic-carpet/	Hardware
Epic Citadel by Unreal Engine	Allows players to explore a medieval landscape and to navigate through a fictional castle realm with various areas such as a circus bazaar, a river and a cathedral.	iOS and Android
Color Band Can be used with: Many Coloured Days by Dr Seuss	Create a picture or draw simple shapes on the iPad, each picture will create a sound when triggered by a hand/arm/body movement which is seen by the camera. A story exploring a variety of different moods linked to a colour.	iOS Book
Intra-personal learning		
Pico Projector	A palm sized LED projector, with 80 to 200 lumens depending on the model chosen. Used to project images/apps/movies into a white tent or onto a white umbrella, to create an individual learning environment. http://www.personalprojector.co.uk/	Hardware
Sphero BB8	An app enabled droid. Controlled by one individual, but perhaps negotiating an evolving obstacle course created by others. http://www.sphero.com/starwars/bb8	Hardware and iOS and Android App
Camera	Taking photographs can be an individual/group activity – for example capturing the story clues on camera during a team treasure hunt activity.	iOS or Android
Inter-personal learning: Technology and apps to support group experiences		
The Adventures of TinTin by Moulinsart	An app depicting the story of TinTin, which presents choices to be made by the group experiencing the story.	iOS and Android

App or tool	What it does	Type
Visual learning experiences		
Opti LED Sensory Projector by Optikinetics	This projector gives users the ability to switch effects on/off and to start/stop the effects wheel using switches. http://optikinetics.co.uk/product-category/projectors/	Hardware
eBooks: Many books have been re-created in apps, which gives us the ability to use large/small scale projection of images during a sensory story.		
Winnie the Pooh	https://itunes.apple.com/gb/app/classic-winnie-the-pooh/id647809786?mt=8	iOS
Nighty Night	https://itunes.apple.com/gb/app/nighty-night-the-bedtime-story-app/id428492588?mt=8	iOS
The Game in the Dark by Herve Tullet	A story about a trip into space. We should not rush to always use complex technology in our sensory stories. It is easy to overlook the impact that magical photoluminescent materials make when lit by an ultra violet torch. Herve Tullet has authored several books, which 'glow in the dark'. On first glance the pages, which also have no words, look blank. Shine an ultra violet torch onto the pages and the story vividly comes to life! https://www.amazon.co.uk/Game-Dark-Tullet/dp/0714864854	Book
The Game of Mirrors by Herve Tullet	Another 'low tech' friendly sensory story. Each page is a reflective, but not perfect, mirror. Simply shine a bright white torch onto the pages to see your reflection. https://www.amazon.co.uk/d/Books/Game-Mirrors-Phaidon/0714866873	Book
The Game of Light by Herve Tullet	https://www.amazon.co.uk/Game-Light-Phaidon/dp/0714861898	Book
Torches	Storytelling with torches would also be enhanced by the use of a white umbrella or tent, to create a small space, with reduced visual and auditory clutter to create a greater focus on the story and its effects.	Hardware
Photoluminescent board	Continuing with the 'glow in the dark' theme, another useful addition to your low-tech toolkit would be a photoluminescent board to create sensory stories. This is the same material which is used to make fire exit signs. Essentially the board stores light, when used with a bright white or ultra violet torch allowing shadows/shapes and outlines to be created on the surface. These are stored briefly, allowing new marks to be made and another strand of the story to be created within moments.	Hardware

Chapter 2

LITERACY

AMY FOLLOWS AND KARA LAWSON

Introduction

This chapter focuses on the way that technology can develop and enhance children's learning in Literacy. Literacy involves many life skills including communicating, listening, reading, writing and social interaction. Incorporating all of these processes into classroom practice can make it challenging to teach, particularly in diverse classroom environments. Effective language skills are fundamental for children to access the curriculum. The Rose Report (2006) highlights the importance of language, not only for accessing literacy, but across the whole curriculum and the child's development. Finding effective strategies to support language and literacy learning while teaching the whole curriculum can be complex. However, creative and effective use of technology can support these learning skills as well as bringing the subject matter to life.

This chapter will present three case studies, and will consider how technology supports teaching and learning within Literacy lessons.

Learning objectives

By the end of this chapter you will:

- understand how technology can support reading and writing;
- know how technology can be used to support communication skills;
- consider the potential for technology to enable learning for pupils with special education needs.

Links to Teachers' Standards

The key standards are outlined below:

S1 **Set high expectations that inspire, motivate and challenge pupils**
Set goals that stretch and challenge pupils of all backgrounds, abilities and dispositions.

S2 **Promote good progress and outcomes by pupils**
Be aware of pupils' capabilities and their prior knowledge, and plan teaching to build on these.

S4 **Plan and teach well-structured lessons**
Impart knowledge and develop understanding through effective use of lesson time.

S5 **Adapt teaching to respond to the strengths and needs of all pupils**
Know when and how to differentiate appropriately, using approaches that enable pupils to be taught effectively.

Have a secure understanding of how a range of factors can inhibit pupils' ability to learn, and how best to overcome these.

Have a clear understanding of the needs of all pupils, including those with special educational needs; those of high ability; those with English as an additional language; those with disabilities; and be able to use and evaluate distinctive teaching approaches to engage and support them.

S7 **Manage behaviour effectively to ensure a good and safe learning environment**
Manage classes effectively, using approaches that are appropriate to pupils' needs in order to involve and motivate them.

Links to National Curriculum Programmes of Study

The case studies presented in this chapter refer to the following content in the National Curriculum:

- Reading comprehension:
  - develop pleasure in reading, motivation to read, vocabulary and understanding by:
    - listening to and discussing a wide range of poems, stories and non-fiction at a level beyond that at which they can read independently;
  - extract meaning from words and text.

- Writing composition:
  - write sentences by:
    - saying out loud what they are going to write about;
    - composing a sentence orally before writing it;
    - understanding the sentence components.
  - planning or saying out loud what they are going to write about;
  - writing down ideas and/or key words, including new vocabulary;
  - selecting appropriate grammar and vocabulary, understanding how such choices can change and enhance meaning;

Case study 1

Pupil learning outcomes

- Read and understand key vocabulary;

- understand how to construct sentences with correct grammar;

- use a wide range of vocabulary to enhance writing quality.

Technology required

- InPrint 3 – symbol software

- iPads with text to speech facilities

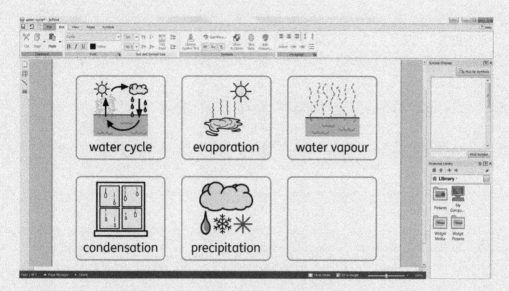

Figure 2.1 InPrint 3 screenshot

A large three-form entry primary school wanted to raise Literacy standards in Key Stage 1 and put different interventions and strategies in place to ensure that good progress was made. Whole-school English assessment analysis showed significant weaknesses with vocabulary, language and sentence construction within all year groups, with Key Stage 1 classes showing significant weaknesses in these areas.

Lesson monitoring, literacy book sharing and environment audits highlighted that each class was using different strategies to teach language and vocabulary. For example, some classes called adjectives 'wow words' while others were using different terminology ranging from 'interesting words', 'describing words' through to 'adjectives'. Through pupil voice group interviews, it was clear that the children were confused due to the terms that the adults were using.

The school decided to implement whole-school approaches to execute a consistent approach to oral language, terminology and visual strategies to teach various areas of Literacy. To ensure that visuals were also consistent throughout the school, the school used a software package called InPrint 3. InPrint 3 creates teaching resources using Widgit Symbols alongside the written word. The school used symbols to label their school environment and produce visual timetables. They also used the software to create visual resources to support teaching and learning across the primary curriculum. There was an agreed list of strategies that each class needed to use consistently on a daily basis:

- label class environment, key learning areas, trays and displays with Widgit Symbols;

- use large visual timetable at the front of the class and individual visual timetables for children who needed additional visual or routine support;

- word banks (for any subject) must display Widgit Symbols alongside the written word;

- use agreed terminology for Literacy and Maths lessons in all lessons (oral and written terminology);

- use Widgit Symbols to support key vocabulary in lessons where the learning objective was not focusing on their reading ability;

- use Colourful Semantics approach to teach sentence construction.

Colourful Semantics is an intervention program devised by Alison Bryan. It is aimed at helping children to develop their grammar but it is routed in the meaning of the words. Colourful Semantics supports sentence construction teaching by breaking down the sentence parts into their thematic roles and then colour codes them. It helps children to organise their sentences accurately as well as develop their language and vocabulary.

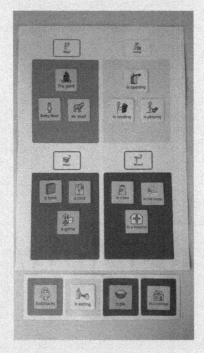

Figure 2.2   Colourful Semantics (using colour-coding)

The school used Colourful Semantics throughout the Foundation Stage and Key Stage 1 classes. Colourful Semantics was also used in Key Stage 2 classes where children still had significant weaknesses with sentence construction. Foundation Stage classes concentrated on using photographs and book illustrations to talk about what was happening in the pictures. Children answered questions like: 'What is the boy doing?' using symbolised multiple choice answers (in the early intervention stages), moving towards answering oral questions with no multiple choice options.

Key Stage 1 classes used two-, three- and four-part sentences within their Literacy lessons to develop the children's sentence construction abilities further. They continued to use Widgit Symbols throughout the school during their Colourful Semantics sessions because it supported the children's understanding of the meaning of the words. Teachers found the symbols useful to visually display the meaning of the verbs they were using within their literacy sessions. More advanced verbs like 'crouch', 'explore', 'collect' were easier to explain and remember due to the visual symbol cue. Teachers also observed that the children were able to independently use the advanced verbs accurately in their writing because they were using the visual display word banks (one of the agreed whole-school strategies).

Symbolised vocabulary lists, information texts and recording sheets were used throughout the school in Maths, Science, History, Geography and RE lessons to support the vocabulary that was being taught. Vocabulary lists were used by the children to help them access information texts and activity questions, and also to help them use the appropriate terminology within their own independent recording.

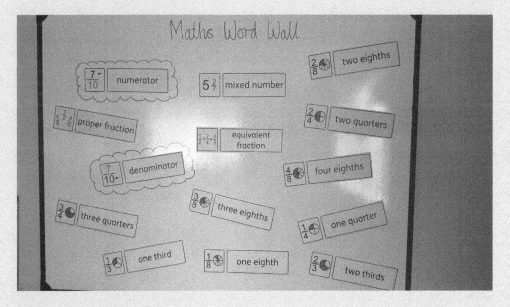

Figure 2.3 Maths word wall

Children had the confidence and self-assurance to work independently as the symbolised resources helped them access the information they required. Children who had additional learning needs also had the ability and confidence to work independently. Some children accessed the symbolised resources on an iPad so they could use the text to speech facilities to read the text to them.

Literacy standards across the school began to improve due to the consistent approaches that had been implemented. Symbolised teaching resources supported the children's ability to access longer texts, which led to stronger text understanding, more advanced vocabulary choices being used in independent writing and improved grammar skills. Writing evidence across the curriculum demonstrated the impact of the consistent approaches. As the symbols were used within all subjects to display key vocabulary and create differentiated activities, children were accurately using the vocabulary within their writing. For example, in one of the Year Three classes, a child with dyslexia enthusiastically wrote about the life cycle of a frog using the correct scientific language. Her level of understanding was commendable and the child said: 'I knew what to write because the pictures (Widgit Symbols) helped me understand what was happening.'

Variations to try

Photographs are also a great way to add visual representation to lesson resources. Children may find it easier to understand the photographs, especially if they are younger. Photographs could be used instead of Widgit Symbols to teach the earlier levels of sentence construction. Photographs of children within different scenarios can make learning more personal.

iPad apps can also support children to creat sentences and some apps have varying levels of embedded support. For example, Clicker Sentences allows you to model the completed sentence before the child uses the app to write the sentence, through to more advanced grid sets where the child chooses words prompted by 'who', 'what doing', 'what' and 'where' to create their own sentences. The Sentence Creator app also supports sentence creation and includes an assessment tracking feature to monitor progress.

Reflective questions

- Consistency throughout a school can support children's learning. Other than oral teaching language, what other literacy areas might need a consistent approach?

- Symbols can support teaching and learning in many ways. How can symbols support children who are on the autism spectrum?

Case study 2

Pupil learning outcomes

- Develop pleasure in reading and motivation to read;

- listen to and discuss a wide range of fiction, poetry, plays and non-fiction;

- explain and discuss their understanding of books, poems and other material.

Technology required: eBooks

This case study focuses on a project with Year 2 pupils. The class was made up of 75 per cent boys and 25 per cent girls, and it had above-average numbers of pupils with special needs. Through a successful bid for external funding (through a local reading charity), the school was able to purchase 30 eBook readers and a collection of eBooks that were used by the whole class every day for seven months. The teacher and Special Educational Needs Co-ordinator (SENCo) had identified in previous reading data analysis that there was a large group of underachieving boys who did not have a love for reading.

The teacher and SENCo planned a wide range of activities through literacy lessons, guided reading sessions and small intervention groups, and also during 'ERIC' (Everybody Reading in Class) time where the eBooks were used to motivate and encourage reading for enjoyment. eBooks were used to support the literacy teaching around different text genres including autobiographies, stories with historical settings, and myths and legends. Guided reading sessions and small intervention groups also provided opportunities to focus on specific groups of children who were underachieving or needed additional reading support.

Figure 2.4 Pupils reading an eBook

For this particular cohort, eleven children with some reading difficulties (which in this instance was 81 per cent boys and 19 per cent girls) who could benefit from the use of eBooks were identified at the beginning of the project. The majority of this identified group were interviewed to discuss their reading routines and their personal views about reading for enjoyment. Of this group, 100 per cent acknowledged that they did not do any reading activities outside of the school day and did not enjoy reading. It was believed by the teacher and SENCo that their reading habits and feelings around reading were the main learning barrier to their reading progress.

The eBooks were implemented across the whole class (including teacher and teaching assistants) to demonstrate and model good practice with reading. Children with reading difficulties were also given access to audio support. The audio support enabled them to access reading books that their peers could access unsupported. This set-up created a magical buzz when the children were reading the main texts linked to their Literacy lessons. All children were eager to continue reading and were highly motivated during Literacy lessons to discuss and explore the texts. As all the children were reading the same text, it created a collaborative environment in which children independently engaged in discussions about the book.

The teacher also observed that the children who were utilising the audio support were able to understand, discuss and express a deeper level of comprehension of the texts they were reading. As the children were not concentrating on using their phonics or decoding skills, they were able to engage more deeply with the text, provoking ideas, discussions, questions and answers.

The use of ICT in this instance enabled a variety of opportunities. It vastly improved the motivation to read, successfully encouraged the children to read for enjoyment, developed children's comprehension skills and improved reading progress across different ability groups.

Variations to try

The range and variety of available eBooks means that they can be used across ages, abilities and subjects. For example, they can be used across the curriculum to enhance learning outcomes, from supporting science lessons with the use of non-fiction information books through to learning to read and speak a modern foreign language.

Cartoons and comic strips are also powerful teaching tools. They can tell a complex story in a few images, provide comment and provoke thought on events and issues in the news, as well as provide identifiable characters to form the basis for character discussions. Cartoons and comic strips can support a wide range of language and discussion activities. They are particularly useful for complex narratives such as Shakespeare.

Reflective questions

The case study school monitored the impact of eBooks for underachieving boys.

* Is this the best way to encourage and motivate underachieving boys?

* What other strategies could have been used to motivate and encourage positive reading relationships?

Case study 3

Pupil learning outcomes

* Plan their writing by discussing and recording ideas;

* draft and write by composing and rehearsing sentences orally;

* record and edit their writing.

Technology required

* Clicker 7 (PC software)

* Clicker Docs (iPad app)

Clicker is a reading and writing tool designed to help pupils of all abilities to achieve rapid and permanent gains in their literacy skills. It is aimed at children from 5 to 11 years old, and at older learners with special needs. The software is specifically designed to support pupils with special/additional needs, including those with dyslexia, learning difficulties, speech or language impairments, and physical disabilities.

The latest version, Clicker 7, provides a child-friendly word processor that can be tailored to support whatever stage of literacy a child is working at, helping every pupil to play an active role in their own learning and offering complete support throughout the writing process. Teachers can also provide differentiated speaking, listening, reading and writing activities on any topic, making Clicker an inclusive tool that can be used across the school for children who are learning to read and write. Clicker 7 has the following support features:

Speech feedback: Each time a sentence is completed, it is automatically read aloud in a clear child's voice. This realistic feedback encourages pupils to punctuate, actively review and self-correct their work. You can also paste any text into Clicker and have it read aloud, giving struggling and emergent readers access to text that they find difficult to read themselves.

Word predictor: Clicker's predictor enables children to give their full attention to what they want to write and encourages them to use more adventurous vocabulary. Use of the word predictor results in greatly improved coherence, spelling and grammar.

Picture support: The CrickPix library contains over 3,500 curriculum pictures to incorporate into documents and activities. Children can also use the painting tools to illustrate their work, or a webcam to take photographs that instantly appear in their documents. This could be used to incorporate images of a science experiment, or pictures of their favourite objects for an 'All About Me' project – a great way to personalise the curriculum.

Voice notes: This tool enables pupils to record their own audio notes before they write. This gives them an opportunity to rehearse their sentences, and offers a powerful way to capture their initial thoughts and ideas. Children can also narrate their own books, practise their speaking skills with a 'Listen and Say' activity, or recount parts of a story in a 'Tell the Story' activity. As recordings are saved as part of a child's work, they can be used as evidence of achievement and, if the task is performed again later, of progress.

Many children within a small primary school were struggling writers. The SENCo wanted to find effective strategies to support and motivate those children who found reading and writing particularly difficult. One difficulty that the school experienced was the varying needs of the children who needed additional reading and writing support. This ranged from children in Key Stage 1 who needed highly scaffolded reading and writing activities, through to children in Key Stage 2 who just needed a word bank to broaden their use of vocabulary.

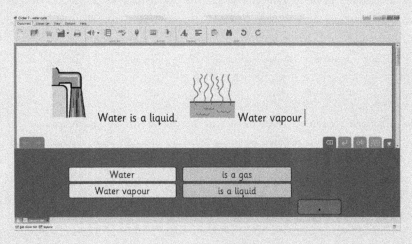

Figure 2.5   Clicker 7 screenshot: water cycle for lower ability children

The school used Clicker 7 to meet the varied needs of the children. They began by using the software program to support writers during their weekly 'big write' sessions. Children used the voice notes to record their ideas into the program. This gave them the opportunity to rehearse their sentences before writing and to adapt or change their ideas. Some of the children who used the voice notes were not confident in their writing ability and found it useful to use the voice notes to experiment and explore different sentences before deciding on which ones to use in their writing. Their confidence, enthusiasm and motivation to write had increased as well as their ability to work independently.

There was a group of children in Year 3 who were very slow at recording their work and needed a lot of adult support to encourage writing. These children were not motivated to write and they found the physical process of writing difficult because they were still developing their physical motor skills linked to writing. The teacher used Clicker 7 for recording within Literacy lessons as well as other subjects across the curriculum including Science, History, Geography and RE. 'Clicker Sets' were quickly set up linked to the lesson subject and the software was tailored to the individual user employing the various template grids within the program.

Some children used the writing grids to organise their sentence structure so that they were able to concentrate on fact-recording within their science lesson about habitats. Other children were able to type into the program to record their ideas. These children used Clicker Docs (iPad app) to widen their vocabulary choices and word prediction to develop their independent spelling skills.

One child within the Year 5 class had complex learning difficulties and used eyegaze technology to communicate. She was able to use her eyegaze communication device to effectively communicate ideas and conversations, but she found her device tricky to use within various subjects because the vocabulary within the device did not meet the language needs of the lesson. Clicker 7 grids were set up for her to access the lesson's subject vocabulary and she used the eyegaze compatibility function of Clicker 7 to access her learning. She was able to write sentences and demonstrate the level of knowledge of understanding that she had acquired during the lesson.

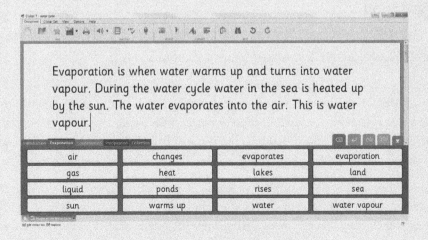

Figure 2.6 Clicker 7 screenshot: water cycle for higher ability children

Children across the school who used the software to support their writing benefited from the level of support the program offers. The pupils were more engaged, focused and willing to persevere within lessons even if they found the task difficult. They began to incorporate more relevant and interesting vocabulary in their written work and used punctuation more consistently than when using a pencil and paper. Several children were also producing longer pieces of writing. Clicker 7 gave the children an alternative way to record their ideas and they demonstrated real enthusiasm when embarking on written tasks that they would normally find difficult and demotivating.

Variations to try

Easi-Speaks are microphones that can record sentences and phrases. They are a useful tool if children need support when constructing ideas and remembering the sentence they just orally constructed. Children's oral language understanding is usually further developed than their reading or writing ability. By listening to their sentence recordings, the children can check that the sentence makes grammatical sense and make changes where necessary before recording them in writing.

Reflective questions

The case study focused on supporting individual reading and writing abilities.

- How could you support collaborative writing when children's abilities vary?

- Which assessment for learning strategies – for example peer assessment – could be supported with technology?

Discussion

Progression

This discussion looks at how the case studies fit into broader schemes of work, the SEN Code of Practice, and EHC needs assessments and plans.

Language is essential in children's learning. It provides them with the means to make sense of the world around them through thought and discussion (Fisher, 1996). Traditionally, symbols were used to support people with communication difficulties such as speech and language disorders. However, the use of symbols is gradually becoming more widespread as teaching professionals realise the benefits they can have for all pupils.

Whole-school approaches to language learning, both mother tongue (first language) and a new language, and the processes of teaching and learning are vital to the coherence of children's experiences during their life in school (DfCSF, 2009). If a whole school implements consistent teaching strategies and uses common terminology, and the approach is understood by all staff, then sustained progression in language learning can happen.

Using symbols throughout a primary school with senior leaders embedding the good practice into whole-school policies will support children's language learning, vocabulary understanding and subject knowledge across the curriculum. Most school-based learning takes place through the spoken and written word. Pupils who experience reading and writing difficulties will face challenges throughout their education. McNamara and Moreton (1990) note that there is a tendency to deliver the curriculum, particularly in history, geography and science, through reading and writing. They found that *it is the very emphasis on reading skills that holds children up in their academic progress* (p.7). Using symbols to support the teaching and learning in these subject areas and across the entire curriculum can help break down reading and writing barriers to subjects.

Even though modern learning technology and other resources have been used to break down these learning barriers, the emphasis on text-heavy lessons still remains in places due to the curriculum knowledge and understanding that is required in various subjects. Writing across the curriculum can be a daily struggle for some students due to the amount of text that is presented to them. James and Kerr (1993) concluded that symbols could be used to enhance the access to text within lessons. One of education's main aims is to give children maximum autonomy in their learning environment. Reading is one of the ways in which this can be achieved. James and Kerr (1993) discovered that by broadening the definition of reading to include the extraction of meaning from symbols, as well as text, such autonomy can be offered to a wider range of children.

The development of literacy is of prime importance. Not only does it underpin many subject areas within the curriculum, it also highlights the importance of using language and communication to find and seek opinion. The SEN Code of Practice (Department for Education, 2015) states that *children have a right to receive and impart information, to express an opinion and to have that opinion taken into account in any matters affecting them from the early years* (p.20). It is important to consider the careful use of technology to gather the opinions of pupils when planning and writing an EHC plan. Their voice needs to be heard and listened to. Pupil voice can be captured through considerate planning and assistive technology to ensure that their honest opinion is shared. Writing grids in Clicker 7 for recording support through to reading pens (pens that scan text and read it aloud) or symbol-supported surveys are a few of the strategies that can be used to enable pupils to express their opinions as part of the EHC planning and reviewing stages.

Differentiation

This section looks at how the approaches can be adapted for different ability groups and areas of need.

As children's literacy support needs vary with age, subject area and specific learning difficulties, differentiation can be challenging. Ensuring that every child is making progress in their learning is a difficult task, but technology enables teachers to facilitate learning to a higher level due to the additional level of support it gives. This is evident in all three of the case studies above.

As noted previously, emergent literacy emphasizes the interrelatedness of reading and writing with both processes acquired concurrently. A growing evidence base supports the use of technology to enhance the development of emergent literacy skills, especially in young learners with additional needs or those who are at risk (Campbell et al., 2006). The process of writing places a variety of demands on the beginning writer, including the difficult task of finding and choosing words. These demands can inhibit the progress of emergent literacy learners.

To minimise these issues and maximise differentiation, many writing programs can present word choices in a grid format, like Clicker 7 in Case Study 3. It is the solid range of support elements and the inclusion of personalised features (Denner et al., 2002) that helps develop stronger connections between the student and the text to increase engagement and comprehension. Creating these stronger bonds between the text and the reader certainly ignites the student's enthusiasm and motivation to concentrate on any given task. Text to speech programs such as Browse Aloud, can support this type of connection within an internet browser. Alongside books, children may encounter difficulties accessing text within internet browsers and social media networks. Encouraging independent browsing is important to ensure that children can access information linked to hobbies, friends and interests. Using the text to speech features while browsing can reduce the barriers between website content and the pupil, enabling a better online experience for them.

Support and challenge

This section explores some ways of scaffolding learning.

The use of digital technology for reading tasks (such as the eBooks in Case Study 2) may increase the motivation and enthusiasm for reading because it opens the eyes of the learners to the content of books as well as other sources. Teachers have observed that learners' use of text to speech increases their love for reading (Andresen, 2007). When children are engrossed within texts, whether assistive technology has been used or not, it allows the teacher to extend the level of teaching and learning because the learners grasp a deeper understanding of the text. Text to speech technology can therefore help children to access a higher level of understanding.

The use of eBooks within primary and secondary classrooms poses interesting questions for teachers to consider. Does it encourage reading for enjoyment? Do they add value to the teaching and learning within the classroom? Picton and Clark's eBook project in 2015 appeared to indicate that boys in particular benefited from taking part in an eBooks project, as there was a higher percentage of boys enjoying reading using technology, reading daily and reading for longer post-project than before they took part. Finding ways to help children enjoy reading more, and motivating them to read more often, has the potential to address longstanding achievement gaps. Children and young people who enjoy reading, and read frequently, are known to be more likely to perform better academically (Picton and Clark, 2015).

Universal Design for Learning to support literacy

Universal Design for Learning (UDL) is an approach that can be used to support literacy by facilitating different types of access and expression through the use of different media. It can be used in conjunction with technology to enhance access to the curriculum for learners, both with and without a Special Educational Need or Disability (SEND). UDL was first introduced in the 1990s (Edyburn, 2015; Rose et al., 2013) and is an educational framework that has its roots in the concept of Universal Design used in architecture (Spencer, 2015; Edyburn, 2015; Rose et al., 2013; King-Sears, 2009; Johnson-Harris and Mundschenk, 2014; Bernacchio and Mullen, 2007). UDL can be defined as:

> *a concept or philosophy for designing and delivering products and services that are usable by people with the widest possible range of functional capabilities, which include products and services that are directly usable (without requiring assistive technologies) and products and services that are made usable with assistive technologies.*

(Section 3 Assistive Technology Act, 1998, pp. 8–9, cited in Spooner et al., 2007, p. 109)

Universal Design for Learning's main aim is to make the curriculum and its content accessible, primarily to learners with SEND, but also to other students who may need help accessing appropriate curriculum content, including students with English as an additional language (EAL), gifted and talented students (G and T) and students outside of the 'average student' (Spencer, 2015). There are three main principles to UDL which can be used to guide teachers in delivering the approach:

1. multiple means of representation;

2. multiple means of expression;

3. multiple means of engagement.

(Edyburn, 2015; Rose et al., 2013; Spencer, 2015)

As an approach, UDL emphasises the need for *accessible pedagogy* (Rose et al., 2013, p. 477), making the curriculum accessible to all learners (Kortering et al., 2008; Johnson-Harris and Mundschenk, 2014) and one way of doing this is through the use of technology in the learning environment.

According to Rose et al. (2013), the UDL framework has similarities with other teaching and learning theories, including Bloom's 2 Sigma Problem and Vygotsky's

Zone of Proximal Development (ZPD). Edyburn (2015) further suggests similarities with Vygotsky's ZPD when he argues that *sustained engagement is achieved by activities that are interesting, motivating and at the right challenge level* (ibid., p. 803). Regarding pedagogy and curriculum content access for learners with SEND, UDL essentially argues that it is not the individual with SEND that is disabled because they experience difficulty in accessing the curriculum, but the curriculum that is disabled for limiting the learner's access to it (Edyburn and Gardner, 2009, cited in Edyburn, 2010). Johnson-Harris and Mundschenk (2014) maintain that UDL is more effective than 'traditional' teaching methods when it comes to accessing the curriculum, because it requires lessons to be designed for learners to access curriculum content from the beginning, pre-emptively and preventatively, as opposed to waiting for the individual 'to fail' and reacting to an individual's needs. It is with these concepts that a paradigm shift needs to occur, regarding the viewpoint of both individual teachers and the wider education system as a whole, for UDL to be effectively implemented across a variety of educational settings. Spencer (2015) claims that the nature of technology is one that is fast-paced and flexible and, as such, this means that it can be used in a variety of different ways and for different purposes. Spencer (2015) and Edyburn (2010) also claim that individual learners need to try lots of different technologies to find where it works for them and where it does not. The fast-paced and ever-changing nature of technology means that there are ever-increasing options for accessing the curriculum that are new and engaging for learners, meaning that the full potential uses for technology within UDL are untapped. However, for technology to be successfully used in conjunction with UDL, King-Sears (2009, p. 201) claims that *technology must be combined with effective pedagogy*.

Summary and Key Points

This chapter has outlined how technology strategies could be used to enable inclusive Literacy learning by addressing attitudes, clearly identifying the needs of the pupils and using appropriate technologies to meet their needs. The range of technology discussed in this chapter can support inclusion in several ways. These include greater learner autonomy, communication support, personalised learning opportunities, higher attainment, motivation and engagement with learning.

It is important to regularly review any strategy to support teaching and learning (including technology) to ensure that the strategy continues to support the individual or group of learners. Technology will not 'solve literacy learning difficulties' but it can enhance, enable and unlock areas of reading and writing which would be inaccessible without the use of technology. Regular reflection and evaluation are essential to confirm that correct strategies are in place to enable learning.

UDL is an approach that aims to create flexible learning environments that accommodate individual learning differences and therefore helps to make literacy more inclusive for a range of learners. UDL serves to make the content accessible through multiple means of representation, expression and engagement to support literacy. The continued advances in the field of technology mean that the opportunities for accessing curriculum content continue to grow and increase the potential for UDL to be utilised in both mainstream and special educational settings.

Useful links and further reading

Abbot, C and Middleton, A (2015) Technology supporting learning, in Lacey, P, Ashdown, R, Jones, P, Lawson, H and Pipe, M (eds) *The Routledge Companion to Severe and Profound and Multiple Learning Difficulties*. London: Routledge, pp. 347–55.

Hardy, C (2000) *Information and Communications Technology For All*. London: David Fulton.

McKeown, S and McGlashon, A (2012) *Brilliant Ideas for Using ICT in the Inclusive Classroom: National Association for Special Educational Needs*. Hoboken: Taylor & Francis.

Rose, DH, Gravel, JW and Gordon, DT (2013) Universal design for learning, in Florian, L (ed.) *The SAGE Handbook of Special Education*. London: SAGE Publications, pp. 475–89.

www.cast.org: website of CAST (Centre for Applied Special Technology), the organisation whose members developed UDL.

www.cricksoft.com/uk/home.aspx: the website for Clicker software.

www.widgit.com: the website for Widgit Symbol software.

References

Andresen, BB (2007) Literacy, assistive technology and e-inclusion, *Journal of Assistive Technologies*, 1(1).

Bernacchio, C and Mullen, M (2007) Universal Design for Learning. *Psychiatric Rehabilitation Journal*, 31(2: 167–69.

Campbell, PH, Milbourne, S, Dugan, LM and Wilcox, MJ (2006) A review of evidence on practices for teaching young children to use assistive technology. *Topics in Early Childhood Special Education*, 26(1): 3–13.

Denner, PR, Rickards, JP and Albanese, AJ (2002) *Generative Learning Effect of the Story Impressions Preview Method on the Comprehension of Information from Narrative Text* (Report No. CS510886). Idaho State University (ERIC Document Reproduction Service No. ED 463541).

Department for Children, Schools and Families (DCSF) (2009) *Developing Language in the Primary School: Literacy and Primary Languages*. London: Department for Children, Schools and Families. Crown copyright.

Department for Education (DfE) (2015) *Special Educational Needs and Disability Code of Practice: 0 to 25 Years Statutory Guidance for Organisations which Work With and Support Children and Young People who have Special Educational Needs or Disabilities*. Available from: www.gov.uk/government/uploads/system/uploads/attachment_data/file/398815/SEND_Code_of_Practice_January_2015.pdf

Edyburn, DL (2010) Would you recognize Universal Design for Learning if you saw it? Ten propositions for new directions for the second decade of UDL. *Learning Disability Quarterly*, 33: 33–41.

Edyburn, DL (2015) Universal Design for Learning, in Spector, JM (ed.) *The SAGE Encyclopaedia of Educational Technology*. Thousand Oaks, CA: SAGE Publications, pp. 802–4. Available from: http://sk.sagepub.com.ezproxy.northampton.ac.uk/reference/download/the-sage-encyclopedia-of-educational-technology/i10368.pdf (accessed 28 May 2017).

Fisher, J (1996) *Starting from the Child*. Buckingham: Open University Press.

James, F and Kerr, A (1993) *On First Reading: Ideas for Developing Reading Skills with Children from Four to Seven*. Twickenham: Belair Publications.

Johnson-Harris, KM and Mundschenk, NA (2014) Working effectively with students with BD in a general education classroom: The case for Universal Design for Learning. *The Clearing House*, 87: 168–74.

King-Sears, M (2009) Universal design for learning: Technology and pedagogy. *Learning Disability Quarterly*, 32: 199–201.

Kortering, LJ, McClannon, TW and Braziel, PM (2008) Universal Design for Learning: A look at what algebra and biology students with and without high incidence conditions are saying. *Remedial and Special Education*, 29(6): 352–63.

McNamara, S and Moreton, G (1990) *Teaching Special Needs*. London: David Fulton.

Picton, I and Clark, C (2015) *The Impact of Ebooks on the Reading Motivation and Reading Skills of Children and Young People: A Study of Schools Using RM Books*. London: National Literacy Trust.

Rose, DH, Gravel, JW and Gordon, DT (2013) Universal Design for Learning, in Florian, L (ed.) *The SAGE Handbook of Special Education*. London: SAGE Publications, pp. 475–89. Available from: http://ebookcentral. proquest.com/lib/northampton/reader.action?docID=1631712&ppg=534 (accessed 28 May 2017).

Rose, J (2006) *Independent Review of the Teaching of Early Reading Final Report*. London: DfES.

Spencer, S (2015) *Sally A. Spencer, Universal Design for Learning*. SAGE Knowledge (online). Available from: http://sk.sagepub.com.ezproxy.northampton.ac.uk/video/sally-a-spencer-universal-design-for-learning (accessed 1 June 2017).

Spooner, F, Baker, JN, Harris, AA, Ahlgrim-Delzell, L and Browder, DM (2007) Effects of training in universal design for learning on lesson plan development. *Remedial and Special Education*, 28(2): 108–16.

Chapter 3

OUTDOOR LEARNING

EMMA WHEWELL AND KAREN WOOLLEY

Introduction

The outdoor environment offers many fabulous learning opportunities that engage and excite the senses. Allowing children to interact with the outdoor environment and to share and capture their journey with others is a powerful tool. Mobile technologies offer children with motor and sensory impairments different ways to experience the physical world. They can become explorers, scientists, treasure hunters, spies and much more beside. This chapter aims to explore learning outdoors with technology and encouraging children to engage with the environment in ways that appeal to multisensory learning, personal development and enjoyment.

Resonating with the work of early years pioneers such as Rousseau and Froebel, there has been a recent resurgence of interest in the UK in the potential of the outdoor environment for supporting children's learning (DfES, 2006). The prominence of outdoor learning in the Early Years Foundation Stage in England and the popularity of Forest School's education (Waite, 2011) demonstrate the increasing recognition of the learning opportunities presented by the great outdoors. Studies have shown that despite outdoor play being recognised as both healthy and desirable, children spend much less time outdoors than they have in previous generations and this is a well-documented cause of reduced physical activity. It is important to consider the impact this may have on their creativity and imaginary play (Back et al., 2016). Combining technology and the outdoors is a potential way of using the appeal and familiarity of computing and gaming with the physical and health-enhancing advantages of the outdoors.

Outdoor learning using mobile technologies can open a number of possibilities for inclusive pedagogies: *tablets have given us a whole new range of possibilities when it comes to children demonstrating their progress and understanding* (Caldwell and James, 2015, p. 29). When learning outdoors children can collaborate to create digital artefacts. The range of apps and tools available is staggering and can offer something for everyone. We have indicated whether the apps we recommend are paid for (££) or free. Johnston (in Kerry, 2011) suggests that learning in the outdoors is most successful when it is:

- child centred;

- practical and exploratory;

- acquired through motivating experiences;

- enhanced through effective peer interaction;

- effectively supported by adult interaction;

- in cross-curricular contexts.

The activities we describe in the case studies below ascribe to this philosophy, and aim to inspire and include all children. This SEND Code of Practice highlights that schools must *foster good relations between disabled and nondisabled children and young people* (DfE, 2015, p.17). The case studies in this chapter offer activities that are appropriate to a range of children, including those with SEND, detailing variations for those who require additional support. They identify the technology required, the possibilities and the adaptions that you may consider to make the task inclusive to the needs of your children.

Learning objectives

By the end of this chapter you should be able to:

- reflect upon a range of technologies that support children with sensory impairments to interact with the physical world;
- explore a range of mobile technology to support children in developing their communication skills;
- identify ways in which technology outdoors can allow children to create and share digital artefacts.

Links to National SENDCo Standards

National SENCO Standards (DfE, 2015)

4. **Strategies for improving outcomes for pupils with SEN and/or disabilities**
    The potential of new technologies to support communication, teaching and learning for children and young people with SEN and/or disabilities.

9. **Develop, implement, monitor and evaluate systems to:**
    Record and review the progress of children and young people with SEN and/or disabilities.

Part C: Personal and Professional Qualities
There are high expectations for all children and young people with SEN and/or disabilities.

Person-centred approaches build upon and extend the experiences, interests, skills and knowledge of children and young people with SEN and/or disabilities.

English: Children use discussion in order to learn; they should be able to elaborate and explain clearly their understanding and ideas.

Science: Children explore and use classification keys to help group, identify and name a variety of living things in their local and wider environment.

Computing: Children are responsible, competent, confident and creative users of information and communication technology.

PE: Children take part in outdoor and adventurous activity challenges both individually and within a team.

PSHE (non-statutory) Children have the skills, language and strategies they need in order to live healthy, safe, fulfilling, responsible and balanced lives.

Case study 1: Making and using trails

Creating trails is an open-ended and flexible way of allowing children to explore the outdoors and to share their experiences with others. Based upon the premise of treasure hunting, mobile technology offers a variety of tools by which children can collect and display information.

Pupil learning outcomes

By making and using trails the children will be:

- exploring familiar and unfamiliar environments with others;

- collaborating with others to design and follow trails;

- creating a digital artefact and sharing their work.

Technology required

To make and create trails, you would need a mobile device with a camera facility, a QR code reader (free) and a photo annotation app such as Pic Collage (free). Accessible technology that would allow visually impaired learners to participate fully include apps such as 'Say It!' (free) which will read text aloud and 'Say Anything' (free) which allows users to enlarge the text available in a scrolling banner. Trail making promotes problem solving and reasoning as well as communication, speech and language. Children share the experience of exploring familiar and unfamiliar environments.

Pic Collage and other photo annotation apps allow users to take pictures of their trail and order, reorder and classify objects. Children can design a trail around a new environment or find natural objects to classify – e.g. colour or shape. Alternatively,

Figure 3.1   Examples of trail making and sorting using Pic Collage

they can use a trail that their peers have made in order to experience their journey or solve their problem.

Creating a shared digital artefact is a powerful way of allowing children to demonstrate their learning, not only in completing or designing the trail, but also in the way in which they have collaborated, shared, communicated and demonstrated many of the soft skills needed when promoting independence, collaboration, tolerance and empathy.

Figure 3.2   Sharing and collaborating builds soft skills

Variations to try

This activity can be varied by using a camera filter, such as that on the Photo Booth facilities (free) or filters on your mobile device. This allows the children to change and manipulate their photo to make their trail more tricky to decipher. It allows black and white, kaleidoscope and X-ray effects to be added to the photo. Similarly, by zooming in on the object in question, the children can photograph perhaps just part of it. The children following the trail have to think differently in order to identify the object or location.

MadPad (£) enables users to create a sound safari that others could follow. MadPad allows the children to record 12 short soundbites. These could be stamping feet or a musical instrument. Once recorded, the children can either follow the sounds in turn or play them like a piano keyboard.

Children could plan their sound safari around the school or grounds recording their sounds, then share this with their peers who have to try to identify the sound, and in turn say what and where the object making that sound is. There is an accompanying video recording that can be used to show what is making the sound if needed. This activity is accessible to children with a visual impairment. MadPad has also been used successfully to record children playing a short musical piece and allows users to all contribute to the end product, which can then be played by layering the sounds one over another, much like they do in a recording studio.

Figure 3.3   QR code link to Technology Outdoors blog

QR code trails offer a simple method by which data, images, text and web links can be stored and subsequently scanned to direct children to collect and use information. Web-based facilities such as classtools.net allow you to create simple QR code trails that can be scanned and followed using a QR code reader (free). Depending upon the purpose and content of the trail, this can range from a simple question/answer treasure hunt that can be read without access to the internet, to a much more sophisticated trail that takes the children to a virtual world of videos and web-based resources (internet access required). This activity can be varied by using a range of settings. QR codes are a versatile resource that can be used indoors and outdoors, with or without internet facilities.

Case study 2: Mapping and recording my journey

Creating digital artefacts together to document and journal their journey is a lovely way of engaging children to take ownership of their purpose and direction of their learning. There are numerous ways of recording your journey. This case study looks at how you might do this using GPS-based apps and alternatively creating a video to accompany your exploration.

Pupil learning outcomes

By mapping and recording their journeys the children will be:

- exploring familiar and unfamiliar environments with others;
- recording their findings in a way that they can share with others;
- beginning to understand orientation and landmarks.

Technology required

To map and record journeys you will need mobile devices with GPS (WiFi or 4G required) and a camera facility. The apps used in this case study are Ramblr and Fotobabble, both of which are free. Ramblr allows the children to record their journeys by adding waypoints to the map using GPS. These waypoints could be a photograph, sound file, video or image which allows their journey to be recorded in a way that is appropriate to their needs. The examples in the image use Ramblr to create artwork using the app. The user decides upon a shape that they would like to make, or follows

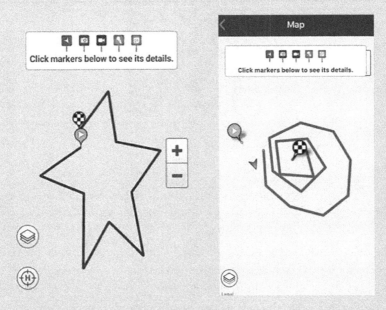

Figure 3.4 Examples of creating art using mapping apps

a pre-designed trail that allows the GPS on the device to track the phone. The children can make a trail or journey that maps on the app as a shape or simple word.

The children need to work together to design their shape and think about when to add a waypoint or to change direction, who will be travelling and how they will do this. They need to choose the way in which they would like to record their journey and how this will be added to their picture. This activity can be done individually or as part of a group, and encourages the children to take ownership of their artwork and route design. Other apps such as MapMyWalk (free) do a similar thing without the ability to add photo and video waypoints.

Variations to try

Fotobabble allows children to add a voice recording to a photograph they have taken in the app. In mapping their journeys it might be a verbal description of the picture, a verbal story board adding a part of a story to the picture, or a clue as to how to find the next marker. This supports speech and language development and collaboration, and is a way for visually impaired children to hear a description of what they are seeing.

Alternatively, a GoPro Camera (££) or camera attached to a child's chair or walking frame can record the child's journey. When using mobile recording devices such as a GoPro camera or drones (££) the children can engage in recording their journeys. By attaching a GoPro, you can alter the angles and, in turn, the way in which you view the world. Simple examples of this might be a welly walk, where the camera is attached to the child's wellies. This allows the child to record their journey or trail, record their ideas and thoughts en route and share it with their peers. GoPros can be used to live stream to another device such as a classroom electronic whiteboard, Apple TV or other mobile device. This allows children outside to share their footage live with another group. This has many possibilities for children collaborating in finding clues, being instructed by the indoor team like a spy, or allowing those children who are not able to leave their classroom or hospital beds to experience the activity alongside their classmates.

Alternatively, options for recording and mapping a journey include the use of drones to record video, live stream to a mobile device or take photographs. Drones give you a bird's-eye view of the world, and inspire awe and wonder in children as it is fascinating to see the world from this angle. Drones are remotely controlled and the children can negotiate with each other perhaps to follow a route or find an object.

Drones can be used in many ways to observe and see the world from a very different perspective. Drone races allow a sense of competition and you can attach robotic hands to some models which would allow activities such as relay races, obstacle courses or tower building. Drones may allow you to film the children completing an activity, such as games in physical education, to allow the children to analyse their movements and contributions.

Drone control does take a little practice and the children would have to be helped to safely control the drones. Apps are available to help the children to learn how to do this. One example is droneSim Pro (free) which allows children to practise on a simulator before they have a go on a very expensive piece of equipment which they might damage. You would also have to take into consideration your environment and whether you have suitable 'air space' for activities such as this. The UK Civil Aviation Authority has clear guidance on the use of drones for fun; guidance can be found at http://dronesafe.uk/. They also offer an app called Drone Assist (free) which allows you to see if you are in a suitable airspace to fly your drone.

Case study 3: Learning about the environment

The outdoors can be a powerful environment for children learning about how to understand and enjoy their role in the ecosystem (DfE, 2013). The science and geography curriculums are very clear in their promotion of hands-on fieldwork, including growing and nurturing plants and vegetables, and interacting with and exploring local environments. This case study offers ways in which technology can enhance children's understanding of flora, fauna and the world around them.

Pupil learning outcomes

By learning about their environment the children will be:

- exploring familiar and unfamiliar environments alone and with others;
- experiencing the natural environment through a variety of media;
- recording what they know about the environment to share with others.

Technology required

The technology used in this case study involves a range of species identification apps. The example given uses Leafsnap free (GPS or Wifi needed), but there are a significant number of species identification apps available on the app stores – for instance, the Royal Society for Protection of Birds has a bird-song recognition app. You could also use the app Fotobabble to enable the children to add speech to their photographs. Leafsnap allows users to photograph a leaf (on a white background) and the app will identify it by shape and then offer users further information about the plant.

This activity supports fieldwork in both science and geography, and allows the children to become explorers. A nature walk to find and identify unfamiliar species is an exciting and enjoyable opportunity. Using the species recognition apps, they are able to successfully discover facts about the flora and fauna. Many of the apps not only show you what you are looking at, but also give you further information such as their fruits and berries, seeds, winter form, etc. Discussions around habitat and food chains allow the children to develop their enquiry and reasoning skills. Why is it here? Who eats it? Why is it this colour? Have you seen it before? Clearly, when exploring any flora and fauna you would expect the same protocols to be in place for any fieldtrip such as hand washing and the countryside code.

Figure 3.5   Using Leafsnap to identify flora and fauna

Variations to try

This activity can be varied by exploring stars in the day or night sky using apps such as Starmap (free), or experimenting with other apps designed to allow the user to identify wildlife such as plants, fungus, lichen and birdsong. The Google Goggles app (free but GPS or Wifi needed) allows the user to take a picture of the object (in this case, wildlife) they wish to perform a search upon, and if the app recognises the object it will provide you with the internet search results, much like a normal internet search. Clearly, the internet is required and alongside it the online safety protocols normally used when performing an internet search. Other apps that are excellent at recognising wildlife include Bird Song Id (£ and requires internet access), which allows users to record birdsong and offers suggestions of the type of bird it might be, and Plantifier (free), which allows users to photograph and identify plants via the app. A number of other apps allow users to identify a host of other flora such as Tree Id, Flower Id and Mushroom Id. Although these are largely designed for flora and fauna in Great Britain, versions are available for other countries.

Reflective questions

- Are there ways in which you could use the technology and activities described to support the needs of the children in your setting?

- Do the technologies and activities described support your assessment practices?

- Are there particular groups of children you can see this working with?

Discussion

By communicating and collaborating on outdoor learning activities the children benefit holistically, both individually and by promoting nurturing relationships with others. In the outdoors children become inquisitive about the environment. From the smells, textures, sounds and visual stimulus they become engaged and excited. There should be no barriers to learning outdoors as it is an incredibly rich resource. Watts (2013, p. 10) suggested that *children seem to respond naturally to the outdoor environment and it is important to ensure that there are additional resources to extend the play.* The resources in our modern society continue to evolve, and technology can enhance and capture experiences for reflection later in the classroom. It can reinforce the learning that has taken place and, in turn, develop digital literacy.

The size and space of the outdoors creates opportunities that cannot be experienced in a classroom: *teaching children outside a classroom, almost regardless of what we are teaching, increases the vitality of learning* (Sedgwick, 2012, p. 3). It excites the senses and inspires the mind. Problem-solving and collaborative skills are developed in enquiry-based learning and the outdoors provides a rich and engaging learning environment where *positive and respectful relationships are modelled, recognised and supported* (Casey, 2010, p. 94).

Table 3.1 Using the STEPPS framework to modify activities (Whewell *et al.*, 2014)

STTEPPS	How can I change provision?	Examples
Space	Would the children benefit from more or less space to complete the learning?	A larger space may be more appropriate for a wheelchair user to negotiate an area/ footpath. A smaller space may benefit a child with a visual impairment in negotiating a trail.
Time	Do some of the children require more time to complete the task or should I split it into smaller parts?	A longer time might benefit those children who take time to absorb new instructions or familiarise themselves with the environment or equipment. A shorter time or smaller chunk of the work may benefit those children who do not have a long attention span or for whom being outdoors would be tiring or cold.
Task	Is the task appropriate for all my children or do I need to offer a variation?	A range of variations to a task is good inclusive practice, but in the outdoors this may include changing the complexity of the task, selecting a more appropriate way of recording the activity, and considering the learning and accessibility needs of your children.
Equipment	Is there a piece of technology that would benefit particular learners?	Visually impaired learners may benefit from using technology that speaks back to them in order to access the task. One example of this would be using 'Say It!' as a means by which they could access the next written clue independently. Children with limited motor skills may benefit from using a larger piece of equipment (iPad instead of iPod) with cases designed to allow children to grip them, attach them to their wheelchairs or frames.
People	How should I organise my class?	Adult support is invaluable for children in the outdoors and consideration must be given not only to the support of the learning taking place but to the pastoral needs of the children in familiar and unfamiliar environments. Peer/buddy support is excellent for promoting collaborative learning and speech and language. Plan your pairs or groups carefully to have a range of skills in your groups.
Pedagogy	How shall I teach my children?	Child-centred learning is important and children will learn many other skills if allowed to explore and problem solve independently. This requires the teacher to plan for a number of eventualities in the learning process. Teacher-centred learning is an important way of showing the children the safe and appropriate ways to use the technology and will be vital in parts of your lesson when teaching outdoors. A combination of both will work well.
Safety	Are the modifications and changes I have made safe?	Off-site activities require a risk assessment to be completed. Make sure that the online safety protocols of your setting have been followed.

Differentiation

Differentiation can be seen as the vehicle that engages all learners at their own level, a consideration of all children's needs and abilities being recognised and catered for individually or in small groups. The activities in the case studies can be adapted for a range of learners. The SEN Code of Practice (DfE, 2015, p. 25) requires that teachers and schools *promote positive outcomes in the wider areas of personal and social development*, and *ensure that the approaches used are . . . having the required impact on progress*. A simple framework that can be used to look at ways to modify your provision is the STTEPPS (Space, Time, Task, Equipment, People, Pedagogy and Safety) framework (Whewell et al., 2014). Table 3.1 demonstrates ways in which you can change an activity depending upon the needs of the learners.

It is important to note that you could make modifications to one element or many elements. It is usual to learn with the children and to think about how you might change activities, knowing your children as well as you do.

Assessment

Assessment in the outdoors is often challenging. You see a huge amount of learning happening but recording it in a meaningful way to report back is sometimes difficult. Assessment should be viewed as a journey of the learning taking place. The case studies in this chapter allow the children to make digital artefacts that could be viewed as the end product (summative assessment). Bringing the digital artefacts back to the classroom following the outdoor learning session can be the focus for a discussion about the children's work. Showcasing their piece and reflecting on the learning is a vital part of the learning journey. The opportunity to demonstrate how they might adapt, change and improve their work demonstrates evaluative and creative skills. By using work produced by the children which details the output – for example, videos or digital artefacts – you can annotate these with evidence of learning. This could include such ideas as the nature of the task, the type of support the child(ren) needed and the successful outcomes in line with good assessment and tracking practice. Savage and Barnett (2017) suggest that technology-enhanced learning (when matched to the children's needs) can offer children alternative ways to express their learning and offer an enabling environment.

But what of the learning taking place during your outdoor session? When children work together they will demonstrate collaborative skills such as turn-taking and listening. You may need to plan in adults to support this and to record their learning happening via video or voice recorder. This recording can then be used as an assessment tool alongside the end product. Plan questions and plenaries throughout your lesson to highlight not only 'good work' but 'good working'. Meaningful assessment of this type of learning is difficult, but when the opportunity arises to record this happening, use the technology on hand to capture these soft skills. Often these are important parts of individuals' Education and Health Care Plans, and group work offers much in terms of social skills and independence. Table 3.2 is adapted from P21 Definitions Framework (The Partnership for 21st Century Learning, 2015), which details the skills and attributes that technology-enhanced learning can offer children. In this case, it has been annotated to represent the opportunities for children with SEND learning in the outdoors.

Table 3.2 Digital learning in the outdoors

Learning and innovation	Digital literacy	Career and life
Collaboration: individually and part of a group and teaching/ sharing with others.	**Programming:** apps, online projects, Raspberry Pi, Scratch.	**Flexibility and adaptability:** working with others in new and unfamiliar environments.
Communication: through discussions, apps, video conferencing from remote/ challenging environments.	**Reporting, reflecting and recording:** articulate the learning using mobile technology in the outdoors.	**Initiative and self-direction:** using technologies to drive towards a final goal with self-application.
Creativity and innovation: creating knowledge using innovative technologies outside the classroom from new and unfamiliar environments.	**Designing and developing:** using the digital artefacts to further learning in the classroom.	**Social and cross-cultural interaction:** develop an awareness of cultural, environmental and SEND differences.
Critical thinking and problem solving: use the outdoor classroom to enhance scenario-based learning.	**Online safety:** understand the limits of the technology outdoors and online safety protocols.	**Productivity and accountability:** use the environment and technology to be proactive and accountable.
Knowledge and understanding: mastery and application in real world learning.	**Sharing:** to share learning using digital technologies – e.g. padlets, blogs, Google Docs.	**Leadership and responsibility:** problem-solving activities promote leaderships and the responsibilities of group working.

Summary and Key Points

This chapter highlights the opportunity for engaging a potentially disengaged generation of children by tempting them into the outdoors with exciting and innovative ways of exploring the world around them. It also looks at ways in which the activities can be adapted to allow children with a range of needs to experience the outside either physically or digitally – for example, allowing children with motor ability impairments new avenues to interact with the outdoors in real time through projecting images and video to a device. Important points to reflect upon are how you can use technology outdoors to enhance not only the subject learning, but also the social skills demanded of the children in working collaboratively to produce digital artefacts and share their learning with others. This includes fostering positive transitions such as to new school environments where learning about the setting in advance or through informal activities could ease anxiety. The activities in this chapter are underpinned by sound pedagogy and research, and prescribe to a socio-constructivist approach to learning where learning and creating knowledge are done most effectively with other children and supporting adults. There is so much potential and innovation in technology outdoors for enhancing learning opportunities. This chapter gives a taster of some of the activities you can offer that are accessible and challenging.

Useful links and further reading

The Digital Leaders Across Boundaries website offers access to an innovative project looking at technology in the outdoors, STEM to STEAM and CLiL. Each year the project runs a massive open online course (MOOC). Available at: http://dlaberasmus.eu/project-overview/

Carina Brage offers many useful ideas for taking technology outdoors alongside further resources. Available at: www.muddyfaces.co.uk/product/teaching-technology-outdoors-by-carina-brage/

The Switched on Range from Rising Stars offers numerous exciting activities to enhance your core subjects, many of which will take you outdoors. Available at: www.risingstars-uk.com/Series/Switched-on-iPad/Products/Switched-on-iPad-Science-1

Helen Caldwell (University of Northampton) has a Pinterest page brimming with ideas for taking learning outside the classroom. Available at: https://uk.pinterest.com/helencaldwel/beyond-the-classroom/

The Faculty of Education and Humanities at the University of Northampton has a technology outdoors blog which details resources and case studies of activities that digital leaders and staff have produced with their partner schools. Available at: https://mypad.northampton.ac.uk/ictoutdoors/

References

Back, J, Heefer, J, Pysander, E, Paget, S, Waern, A (2016) Designing children's digital-physical play in natural outdoors settings. Available at: www.diva-portal.org/smash/get/diva2:920536/FULLTEXT01.pdf

Caldwell, H and Bird, J (2015) *Teaching with Tablets*. London: SAGE.

Casey, T (2010) *Inclusive Play: Practical Strategies for Children from Birth to Eight* (2nd edn). London: SAGE.

Civil Aviation Authority: www.caa.co.uk/Consumers/Model-aircraft-and-drones/Flying-drones/ (accessed 18 May 2017).

Department for Education (DfE) (2013) *National Curriculum*. Available at: www.gov.uk/government/collections/national-curriculum (accessed 18 May 2017).

DfE (2015) *Special Educational Needs and Disability Code of Practice: 0 to 25 years*. London: Department for Education. Crown copyright.

Kerry, T (ed.) (2011) *Cross-Curricular Teaching in the Primary School*. London: Routledge.

Savage, M and Barnett (2017) *Technology-enhanced Learning in the Early Years Foundation Stage*. St Albans: Critical Publishing.

Sedgwick, F (2012) *Learning Outside the Primary Classroom*. Oxford: Routledge.

The Partnership for 21st Century Learning (2015) P21 Framework Definitions: available at: www.p21.org/storage/documents/docs/P21_Framework_Definitions_New_Logo_2015.pdf (accessed 15 May 2017).

Waite, S (2011) *Children Learning Outside the Classroom from Birth to Eleven*. London: SAGE.

Watts, A (2013) *Outdoor Learning through the Seasons: An Essential Guide to the Early Years*. London: Routledge.

Whewell, E, Woolley, K and Kellam, R (2014) Physical education (Chapter 11), in Smith, P and Dawes, L (2014) *Subject Teaching in Primary Education*. London: SAGE.

Chapter 4

MUSIC TECHNOLOGY

NEIL SMITH AND JENNI SMITH

Introduction

Music has a unique ability to capture the attention of all students, including those with severe learning difficulties (SLD) and profound and multiple learning difficulties (PMLD). Even children with hearing impairments seem to be drawn to rhythms felt through vibrations.

Music can be part of a holistic educational approach for SLD and PMLD students. Encouraging students to recognise and react appropriately to changes in music can promote cognition. Interaction with others to create music can feed into the Personal, Social and Health Education (PSHE) curriculum with awareness of others and turn-taking.

Music can be used to improve the communication skills of PMLD students. Ockelford et al. (2002) stated that young people with PMLD are still in the very early stages of development that is equivalent to the first year of 'typical' development. Although these young people are unlikely to follow a 'typical' developmental path, there are likely to be parallels with early infant development. The importance of music in the development of communication was suggested by Trevarthen (2000) who showed how musicality is used in early interactions between parents and infants. The musicality leads to cooperative awareness which promotes the social bonding which is necessary to establish communication. Brandt et al. (2012) reviewed studies of music and language, and suggested that musical hearing and ability is essential in the acquisition of language. Recent neuroscience studies (Cumming et al., 2015) have shown an overlap in the processing of music and language syntax within the brain. With this in mind, music is clearly an important part of any PMLD curriculum. Ockelford (2000) noted how music can encourage vocalisation and that young people with learning difficulties start to communicate through rhythmic structure even though they can't use words. Wheeler and Stultz (2008) found that music could promote a child's ability to self-regulate and attend, which are both necessary prerequisites for effective communication.

Music can be used with SLD and PMLD students as an important tool for learning within lessons rather than being taught as a separate subject. In this context, the students' ability to communicate and interact with the world around them are important objectives within the lessons.

The sounds of intent framework (Ockelford, 2015) gives a theoretical underpinning for how music can supplement and support a student's communicative abilities. We discuss that framework at the end of the chapter.

Technology is an important method of enriching music education for SLD and PMLD as it allows students to create music that is more than percussion. Most students will be able to make deliberate sounds with a drum, chime bells, or bells strapped to a wrist or ankle, but the technological music players allow students to create music with melody and different tones without requiring high levels of technical skill or manual dexterity. For this reason, the inclusion of technology in music-based lessons can powerfully enrich the student experience.

Learning objectives

By the end of this chapter you should be able to:

- describe how music can be used to develop communication skills for SLD and PMLD students;
- demonstrate how technology can be used to enhance learning of music and communication with SLD and PMLD students.

Links to Teachers' Standards

The key standards are outlined below:

S1 Set high expectations which inspire, motivate and challenge pupils
Set goals that stretch and challenge pupils of all backgrounds, abilities and dispositions.

S2 Promote good progress and outcomes by pupils
Be aware of pupils' capabilities and their prior knowledge, and plan teaching to build on these.

S4 Plan and teach well-structured lessons
Impart knowledge and develop understanding through effective use of lesson time.

S5 Adapt teaching to respond to the strengths and needs of all pupils
Know when and how to differentiate appropriately, using approaches which enable pupils to be taught effectively.

Have a secure understanding of how a range of factors can inhibit pupils' ability to learn, and how best to overcome these.

Have a clear understanding of the needs of all pupils, including those with special educational needs; those of high ability; those with English as an additional language; those with disabilities; and be able to use and evaluate distinctive teaching approaches to engage and support them.

Links to National Curriculum Programmes of Study

The case studies presented in this chapter refer to the following content in the National Curriculum:

Key Stage 1 pupils should be taught to:

- use their voices expressively and creatively by singing songs and speaking chants and rhymes;
- play tuned and untuned instruments musically;
- listen with concentration and understanding to a range of high-quality live and recorded music;
- experiment with, create, select and combine sounds using the inter-related dimensions of music.

Key Stage 2 pupils should be taught to:

- sing and play musically with increasing confidence and control;
- use their voices and playing musical instruments with increasing accuracy, fluency, control and expression;
- listen with attention to detail and recall sounds with increasing aural memory;
- appreciate and understand a wide range of high-quality live and recorded music.

Case study 1: Soundbeam

The Soundbeam device (described more fully below) uses ultrasonic distance sensors to enable students to control music and sound generation. The non-contact nature of the sensors allows a wide range of students to interact and control the making of music and sounds. This can be useful in a wide range of contexts. With PMLD students, the Soundbeam can be used to develop their understanding so that they can start or stop activities through their movements, or choose different stimuli. Other students can use the device to communicate more purposefully and in a group context. For many students, the Soundbeam offers an exciting way to engage in musical performance (whether solo or in a group) without requiring great technical skill on an instrument.

The development of this case study was informed by the Sounds of Intent Framework (Ockelford, 2015) and the Routes for Learning Assessment Framework (Department for Education, 2015). Sounds of Intent was used to assess the student's progress across a range of criteria.

Learning outcomes

This case study describes a plan of single-student activities for a PMLD student. The student used the Soundbeam device to develop their communicative and cognitive abilities. The learning difficulties of this student required that the activities be repeated and developed slowly over a series of lessons.

Over the series of lessons, the student should be able to show:

- awareness of different stimuli and awareness of other people working with them;

- understanding that their movements can start, stop or alter an activity (such as a sound or music sample);

- purposeful interaction with objects;

- anticipation of a stimulus;

- ability to communicate like and dislike of a stimulus and preference for how (or whether) it should continue;

- interaction with others using sound.

The Soundbeam device

Soundbeam (available at: www.soundbeam.co.uk) is a commercial product that allows disabled people to create sounds. It comprises a dedicated controller, ultrasonic sensors to detect movement and optional wireless press-switches. The ultrasonic sensors are sensitive to movement around them. When they detect movement, the Soundbeam plays a pre-programmed sound (or sound sequence). The sounds can also be triggered by the press-switches or through the controller's touch screen. The controller's touch screen can also be programmed to display images or animations in response to the input, and the controller can be connected to a projector.

Because the ultrasonic sensors detect movement, the student need not move in a particular way or press a target in order to create sounds. This means that it can be suitable for children with severe movement problems, as even unrefined movements can give useful and predictable results.

Lesson series outline

This case study was developed for a PMLD student who was developing their skills at initiating communication and interaction. The student was being supported in developing their communication and other interaction skills by all staff they were in contact with, through exploration of carefully considered challenges.

The lessons in this case study proceeded in a cumulative fashion, with the activities developing on the progress and behaviours demonstrated in each session. The Soundbeam was used as one musical device in the lesson, with the student also having access to a set of chime bells at different times. The teaching staff used a variety of other devices and instruments, such as chime bells, a saxophone and digital music players.

The student was positioned near the Soundbeam device so they had to move their arms to activate the beam, generating and stopping sounds. At first, the student's spontaneous arm movements were sufficient to activate the Soundbeam; staff encouraged the student in these movements and emphasised the causal link between the student's movements and the effects on the sound. As the student progressed, the positioning of the Soundbeam and student were adjusted so that the student had to make more deliberate and purposeful movements to activate the Soundbeam.

Different pre-set sounds were tried on the Soundbeam and those that elicited the greatest response were used in subsequent lessons. When staff interacted with the student using other instruments, the same instrument was used for each particular sound set (e.g. saxophone with April Blues) to encourage recognition and anticipation.

At first, the interactions were initiated by the staff, while being aware of the student's reaction to them. Once the student showed signs of linking their movement to the sounds that the Soundbeam produced, staff would introduce sounds on their devices, such as a backing track to help encourage music making. As the sessions progressed, the interactions became more guided by the student's expressions of sentiment and communicative acts, such as signalling more, less, faster, or quieter sounds and music. Later in the sessions, the student displayed more understanding of others. This was developed by staff initiating turn-taking with staff playing a motif on their instruments and giving the student time to respond using the Soundbeam.

Variations

The Soundbeam is a flexible device that can be used for a variety of purposes. The most obvious is as a musical instrument, where a student uses the Soundbeam to perform. However, depending on the abilities of the student and their developmental needs, it can be used for different purposes. This example shows how the Soundbeam can be used to promote interaction and communication with other people, through the medium of controlling music and expressing desires for others' music and sound creation to change.

Case study 2: Skoog

The Skoog (available at: http://skoogmusic.com) is a large and robust controller for making music. Physically, it is a cube about 20cm on a side with protrusions on five sides. It connects via Bluetooth to a nearby device (iOS, PC or Mac, but not Android) which runs the controller app. While the Skoog appears to have a range of coloured buttons on its surface, the whole surface is sensitive and detects different levels of pressure intensity on any side. Depending on the needs of the student, the Skoog can be placed on their lap, on the floor within reach, or on a separate stand near the student.

In the controller app, a teacher can set up how sounds are generated in response to pressure and touch on the Skoog. This allows for a range of responses and different music to be played. In a SEND setting, the controller can set appropriate pressure levels required for the student to activate the device. For some students, the pressure threshold can be high to ensure that only deliberate actions trigger sounds; for others, the pressure threshold can be low so that even small movements generate a response, which can prompt further interaction.

Figure 4.1   The Skoog

If the teacher prepares the sounds generated for the Skoog, choosing notes on a pentatonic scale will ensure that whatever notes the student plays will sound concordant.

With the Skoog, the controller app is usable by some SLD students. The app is easy to use and the instruments and backing tracks in the app are identified by pictures. A useful feature of the Skoog is the ability to record students' vocalisations. These captured sounds can be modified in the Skoog controller, such as by shifting the pitch. The different sounds can then be associated with different activations of the Skoog, such as having a different pitch playback triggered by each side of the Skoog. This allows students the ability to create music with their own sounds.

Learning outcomes

This case study describes a plan of student activities for a mixed-ability group of PMLD and SLD students. Similar to Case study 1, the objective of the lessons was to develop students' communication and cognitive skills through music. For some of the more able students, the objective was to develop their appreciation of music directly and their ability to create music in a group. Some students used Skoog devices, while others used more traditional instruments such as chime bells. The learning difficulties of some of the students required that the activities be repeated and developed slowly over a series of lessons, while for more able students the musicality could be developed over time. All students received significant one-to-one attention from staff during the sessions, along with work in small groups and the whole group.

The learning outcomes for PMLD students are fundamentally the same as for Case Study 1 above – mainly, the appreciation of cause and effect. For SLD students, over the series of lessons, the students should be able to show:

- turn-taking and interaction within staff and other students;

- recognising changes in rhythm, tempo and dynamics, and making appropriate musical responses;

- using the Skoog app to choose their preferred backing tracks, instruments and sounds for playing later (an IT outcome);

- recording their own vocalisations with the Skoog app and assigning them to Skoog buttons for playing (an IT outcome);

- socialising and interacting with others and taking part in group activities (a PSHE outcome);

- PSHE: socialisation and interacting with others, taking part in group activities.

Lesson series outline

When the students are first introduced to the Skoog, the sounds should be simple to allow the students to simply explore the feel of the device and experience interactions with it. The intention of early sessions is purely to make the student familar with the Skoog and understand that sound production is caused by their manipulation of the Skoog.

Other instrument sounds can be introduced as the student becomes more familiar with how the Skoog operates. As a student becomes familiar with the Skoog over the course of the sessions, its settings will likely become more personalised for that student.

Staff should introduce backing tracks into the room as often as possible. A backing track with a good beat is useful for engaging students' attention on the music and activity in the room. The beat can also act as a cue for the more able students to play their Skoog or other instrument.

Each session should start with a round-robin welcoming song. Each student will have an appropriate instrument, including Skoog. The teacher can sing (perhaps with a backing track) a simple introduction phrase such as *Welcome Jack, welcome Jack, what can you play?*, then invite the appropriate student to play something on the instrument.

The bulk of each session can explore different songs with different tempos, rhythms and dynamics. The teacher can lead each tune with the students making their own contributions to the music. Staff should encourage students to make their contributions appropriate to the changing nature of the music, such as encouraging the students to come in on certain cues or to play notes in time.

When starting the sessions, or with less able students, the teacher can echo the student's musical contribution back to them on the teacher's instrument (or voice, singing back). The teacher should encourage the student to recognise that the student's own contribution has been repeated to them.

The Skoog app can also be used by staff or students to create individualised music. Initially, the music should be played back to the student immediately to further reinforce that the student's creations have musical merit. Staff can then edit it to select a particularly apposite sound or phrase. This can be added to the Skoog's repertoire for the student to play back later. As a student builds up a collection of such samples, they can use them to create much more individualised music in later sessions.

As this session sequence is based around music, the Sounds of Intent assessment framework is more appropriate here than in Case Study 1.

Variations

The Skoog is easily used in proximity with other students, as the requirement for direct touch reduces the chances of other students triggering sounds. (Devices such as the Soundbeam are susceptible to accidental triggering by others.) This allows the Skoog to be used more easily in a group setting with more mobile students, each making sounds in their own way.

As mentioned above, the Skoog controller app is easy to use, and some SLD students will be able to select, process and use sounds themselves with the app. Other students may need to direct a member of staff to control the app, while still making decisions about which clips are used and how.

Reflective questions

- What role does music play in the lives of people with SLD and PMLD?
- How can music and sound be used as a cue for interaction or other activity?
- How can engagement with creating music lead to development in other areas, such as communication and interaction or physical control and development?

Discussion

Music and communication

Music need not be used just for music appreciation. As the case studies showed, music can be used to promote communication and interaction with other people. Music can also be used in the context of multi-sensory sessions for SLD and PMLD students. For instance, music can be used as a cue for other activities starting or finishing, or to introduce themes and events in a story being told.

Music can also allow students to express themselves more effectively, especially if they have problems with speech or signing. Technology can be useful in that context, as devices such as the Soundbeam, Skoog and Wekinator (see below) can allow students to make pleasant sounds, or the unpleasant sounds they intend, without the need for physical expertise or technical skill to use a traditional instrument. In addition, specialised devices such as the Soundbeam and Skoog can be easier for students to use than, for example, an iPad app which requires sufficient dexterity to use a touchscreen.

Sounds of Intent

Sounds of Intent (Ockelford, 2015) is a framework for assessing and promoting the musical development of children and young people with learning difficulties. It was initially developed with reference to SLD and PMLD children.

Sounds of Intent (SoI) accommodates the varied needs and abilities of SLD and PMLD learners by assessing them in three independent domains: reactive (listening and responding to sound and music), proactive (making sound and music), and interactive (engaging, not necessarily creating, sound in the context of other people). Each of these domains has six levels, ranging from no awareness to an understanding of groups of sounds, to an awareness of the emotional content of music. While these levels will tend to correlate across the domains, there is no particular ordering between them.

SoI is an assessment framework. When a student's current abilities need to be assessed, each instance of their musical behaviour is categorised by the SoI domain and level. These events are averaged for each domain and the results plotted on a graph. In subsequent sessions, the assessment can be repeated and the new result plotted. The graph, over time, gives an insight into the student's progress.

A particular feature of SoI is its focus on music and musicality. Case Study 1, above, used SoI as an assessment framework for a more general understanding of how communication developed in a PMLD student, where music was the medium for the communication, not the main focus of the sessions. In this role, SoI was less useful than it would have been for a case study concentrating on the development of musical skills.

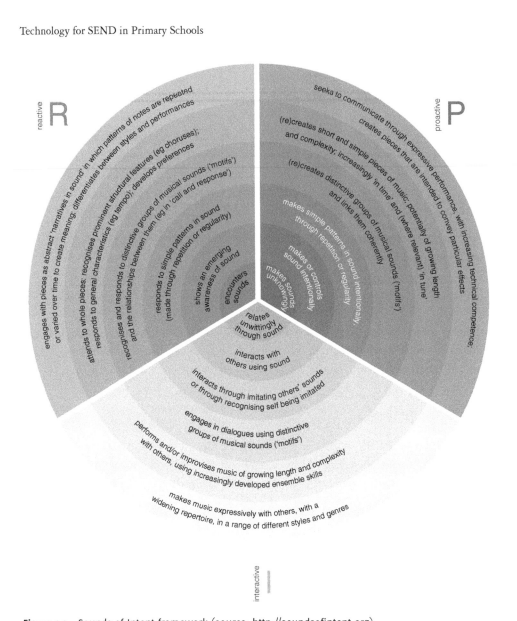

Figure 4.2 Sounds of Intent framework (source: http://soundsofintent.org)

The Routes for Learning framework (Department for Education, 2015) is more specific to the assessment of communication and cognitive development, but is less useful than SoI for cataloguing ability at the lower range of PMLD students. In contrast, Case Study 2 has a greater emphasis on music, so the SoI framework is more appropriate for that style of lesson and that ability of student. Teachers should choose which assessment framework is most appropriate for their students and the learning objectives of the sessions.

As Ockelford himself notes, early indications of progress in the SoI assessment can be misleading due to various elements of increasing familiarity: an assessor new to SoI becoming more familiar with the assessment tool, an assessor new to the student becoming more familiar with the student and their foibles, and the student becoming more familiar with the particular tasks in the scheme of work. This is a drawback of most assessment frameworks and should be kept in mind whenever a new framework is adopted or applied.

> ## Summary and Key Points
>
> Music and soundmaking can be an important part of special needs education. Music can act as a great motivator and attention-grabber for many students, helping teaching staff engage the students in the other activities in the lesson. Musical cues can introduce or foreshadow events or activities, again promoting engagement and anticipation.
>
> Music can be a powerful part of an holistic approach to special needs education. Recognising and responding to changes in music can develop cognitive skills, expressing desires about music, as well as creating music and promoting communication. Interacting with others, perhaps in a group setting, can develop PSHE-related abilities.
>
> As these case studies have shown, music can also be used to promote general cognitive and communicative skills in SLD and PMLD students. The music can engage the student in the activity. The ability of devices like the Soundbeam and Skoog to create high-quality and appropriate sounds and music allows students to make authentic contributions to an ongoing musical activity.
>
> Assessment frameworks such as Sounds of Intent and Routes for Learning provide a clear structure and guidance for how students' ability and progress can be evaluated and recorded. This can feed into general recording of progress, such as P-levels for more able students, or whatever progress recording framework is used in your school.

Useful links and further reading

Optibeam

The Optibeam (http://optimusic.com/optibeam) device is similar to the Soundbeam. Optibeam, however, uses light beams to control the music. Coloured light beams come from a central projector. Students can control the music by either reflecting the beam back to the projector, or breaking a beam that is set up to statically reflect. The controller connects to a PC which plays sounds or music in response to the changing light beams, in a very similar manner to the Soundbeam.

The light reflectors enable a wider range of students to use the device. Even PMLD students with very limited movement can participate in activities; if the reflector is carefully placed somewhere on their body, they will be able to interact with the device with even small movements of the appropriate body part.

The larger number of sensor beams, compared to the Soundbeam, means that richer interactions are possible. For more able students, the multiple beams can be associated with multiple notes, turning the Optibeam into something like a traditional instrument. The larger number of sensors also makes the Optibeam more suitable for group settings, with each participant controlling some of the beams.

Figure 4.3 Optibeam

The Wekinator

The Wekinator (http://www.wekinator.org) is a more flexible version of the Soundbeam which requires more technical expertise to set up. The Wekinator is a software package that runs on a PC. Sensors are connected to the PC; these can include the keyboard and mouse, but can also be motion sensors, ultrasonic movement sensors, tilt switches, and so on. The Wekinator's outputs can be sound samples or generated using a built-in software synthesiser.

Once the sensors are connected and the outputs determined, the teacher/operator *trains* the Wekinator to associate different inputs with different outputs. When the input is repeated, the same output is generated. What makes the Wekinator interesting is that inputs similar to the trained one give outputs that are similar to the trained one. For instance, one could train the Wekinator to give a high pure tone on the software synthesiser when there is something close to a distance sensor, and a low rough tone when things are distant. Once trained, when the distance changes, the tone generated will vary smoothly between the two extremes and could well continue to vary outside them.

This approach gives great flexibility for how the Wekinator and sound are used with students. A wide variety of devices can be used as inputs, even if they are not the standard ones in kits like the Soundbeam. The disadvantage is that there is generally more work involved in getting them working, as the inputs need to be connected to the PC. This can be technically demanding, especially if the proposed input device is non-standard.

References

Brandt, A, Gebrian, M and Slevc, LR (2012) Music and early language acquisition. *Frontiers in Psychology*, 3(327).

Cumming, R, Wilson, A, Leong, V, Colling, LJ and Goswami, U (2015) Awareness of rhythm patterns in speech and music in children with specific language impairments. *Frontiers in Human Neuroscience*, 9(672).

Department for Education (DfE) (2015) Routes for learning. Available at: http://complexneeds.org.uk/modules/Module-2.4-Assessment-monitoring-and-evaluation/All/m08p010a.html (accessed 21 August 2017).

Ockelford, A (2000) Music in the education of children with severe or profound learning difficulties: Issues in current U.K. provision. A new conceptual framework, and proposals for research. *Psychology of Music*, 28: 197–217.

Ockelford, A, Welch, G and Zimmermann, S (2002) Focus of practice: Music education for pupils with severe or profound and multiple difficulties — Current provision and future need. *British Journal of Special Education*, 29(4): 178–82.

Ockelford, A (2015) The sounds of intent project: Modelling musical development in children with learning difficulties. *Tizard Learning Disability Review*, 20(4): 179–94. DOI: 10.1108/TLDR-02-2015-0007.

Trevarthen, C (2000) Musicality and the intrinsic motive pulse: Evidence from human psychobiology and infant communication. *Musicae Scientiae*, 3(1): 155–215.

Wheeler, BL and Stultz, S (2008) Using typical infant development to inform music therapy with children with disabilities. *Early Childhood Education Journal*, 35: 585.

Chapter 5

SCIENCE

HEATHER GREEN AND DEBORAH WILKINSON

Introduction

This chapter focuses on the way that Information Communication Technology (ICT) can enhance children's learning in science. During science lessons, teachers need to develop children's process skills (the doing of science) so that they can approach their explorations of the world in a meaningful way and develop their conceptual understanding (the knowledge and understanding of science). The process skills of working scientifically encompass observing, posing questions, developing hypotheses, making predictions, planning investigations, gathering evidence, interpreting evidence, considering explanations, and communicating results and conclusions (DfE, 2013). The effective use of ICT can support these process skills as well as helping to secure progress in conceptual understanding. Used successfully, computers can aid children's communication skills. The key idea here is to exploit the 'C' in the communication part of ICT, and computers can enable children to share their understanding of science concepts through the use of written reports, video or audio clips, e-mail, blogs or social media. Data loggers, cameras, video or digital microscopes are other tools that can help children to capture their observations during an investigation, and can also be referred to (an aide-memoire) when communicating findings, interpreting data and drawing conclusions. The interactive whiteboard can be used to introduce problems to children, store information (children's questions, concept maps and word banks) that can be referred to over a unit of work, as well as being used as a collaborative tool for sharing ideas. Finally, online games are a powerful way to consolidate learning of science concepts.

This chapter will present three case studies and will discuss how ICT helped children with a range of special needs to work scientifically while developing their conceptual understanding.

Learning outcomes

At the end of this chapter you should be able to:

- know how ICT can engage children in the process of working scientifically;
- know how ICT can support conceptual understanding of science concepts;
- know how ICT can be used to support communication skills.

Links to Teachers' Standards

There are a number of links between ideas presented in this chapter and the Teachers' Standards, but the key ideas are bullet pointed below:

- S2 Promote good progress and outcomes by pupils.
- S3 Demonstrate good subject and curriculum knowledge.
- S4 Plan and teach well-structured lessons.
- S5 Adapt teaching to respond to the strength and needs of all pupils.
- S7 Manage behaviour effectively to ensure a good and safe learning environment.

(DfE, 2011)

Links to the National Curriculum Programmes of Study

The case studies presented in this chapter refer to the following content in the National Curriculum:

- Science

  - Year 1 – identify and name a variety of common wild and garden plants, including deciduous and evergreen trees.
  - Year 5 – to compare everyday materials on the basis of their properties (thermal insulators).
  - Year 6 – use recognised symbols when representing a simple circuit diagram.

- Computing

  - Select, use and combine a variety of software (including internet services) on a range of digital devices to design and create a range of programs, systems and content that accomplish given goals, including collecting, analysing, evaluating and presenting data and information (DfE, 2013).
  - Use technology purposefully to create, organise, store, manipulate and retrieve digital content (DfE, 2013).

Key stages 1 and 2:

Through a variety of creative and practical activities, pupils should be taught the knowledge, understanding and skills needed to engage in an iterative process of designing and making. They should work in a range of relevant contexts – for example, the home and school, gardens and playgrounds, the local community, industry and the wider environment.

When designing and making, pupils should be taught to:

Key Stage 1

Design

- generate, develop, model and communicate their ideas through talking, drawing, templates, mock-ups and, where appropriate, information and communication technology;

Evaluate

- evaluate their ideas and products against design criteria;

Technical knowledge

- explore and use mechanisms – for example, levers, sliders, wheels and axles – in their products.

Key Stage 2

Design

- use research and develop design criteria to inform the design of innovative, functional, appealing products that are fit for purpose, aimed at particular individuals or groups;
- generate, develop, model and communicate their ideas through discussion, annotated sketches, cross-sectional and exploded diagrams, prototypes, pattern pieces and computer-aided design.

Case studies

Although the following case studies are based around SEND, they could be used in mainstream school, as good teaching enables all to reach potential. As Dyson (1990) suggests: *Special educational needs are needs that arise within the educational system rather than the individual, and indicate a need for the system to change further in order to accommodate individual differences.* Dyson's ethos is underpinned by the principles set out in The SEN Code of Practice (2014), which maintains that *mainstream schools must ensure that children with SEN engage in the activities of the school alongside pupils who do not have SEN.* The Code of Practice also describes inclusive practice that *makes high quality provision to meet the needs of children and young people* (DfE, 2015). In addition to the Code of Practice, the inclusion statement maintains that teachers should set suitable challenges and high expectations for every pupil. They should respond to pupils' needs and overcome potential barriers for individuals and groups of children. Lessons should be planned to ensure that there are no barriers to every pupil achieving. In many cases, such planning will mean that these pupils will be able to study the full national curriculum (DfE, 2015). The case studies provide examples of engaging activities suitable for meeting a wide range of needs, enabling every pupil to study the full Science curriculum.

Case study 1: Exploring thermal insulation

This unit of work was presented to a class of Year 5 children who had moderate learning difficulties, part-way through a unit of work relating to properties of

Figure 5.1 Artefacts used to stimulate curiosity

materials. In order to stimulate curiosity at the beginning of the lesson, part of the classroom had been cordoned off using tape. Behind the tape were a number of artefacts including a 'freeze ray' and a brown box (containing Minions frozen in ice and a letter (Figure 5.1).

The artefacts stimulated interest from the children and they were keen to know what was in the box. The box was opened and the following letter was read to the children.

Hello All,

I have a problem – my Ice Ray has malfunctioned and it does not seem to freeze things brilliantly. Watch the video to see how it should work.

You see, I need to keep objects trapped in ice for as long as possible so that I can escape should I need to. Dr Nefario has said that the Ice Ray cannot be repaired but that it should be possible to stop the ice from melting too quickly.

Talk about how you might do this – Dr Nefario has provided an ideas sheet to help you to think about some ideas.

Good luck,

Gru

At the beginning of the lesson the children watched a short video clip on the IWB from the film *Minions* so that they can see what the function of a freeze ray was. This was undertaken so that all children were able to access the lesson (even if they had not seen the film). After paragraph 2 of the letter was read to the children, they were asked what they thought the problem was that Gru wished them to solve – the need to stop ice from melting too quickly. The final part of the letter directed children to an ideas sheet (Figure 5.2) to stimulate discussion and to inform the planning process by establishing the answer to the question 'Which material would be the most effective to wrap around the ice to stop it melting?'

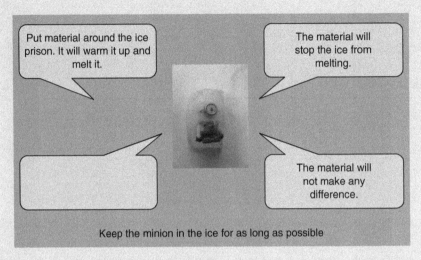

Figure 5.2   A tool to stimulate talk

The concept cartoon was developed from the work of Naylor and Keogh (2000).

Children were provided with a number of different types of materials which they wrapped around the ice in order to observe which material was 'best' to stop the ice from melting (if children have poor motor control you could consider using different types of socks).

ICT was used both during and after the data-collection process to support with observational skills, presentation of findings and interpreting data. Over a period of 15–20 minutes, the children observed the ice cubes and used cameras to take photographs of their findings in order to encourage them to observe the amount of liquid water in each condition and to focus on the task. In addition to this, children were provided with Talking Tins so they could orally describe what they had observed. This served to remind them of what happened during the investigation and could be replayed when communicating their findings in a written form. As children could only record a few sentences on the Talking Tin, they had to think carefully about what they wanted to say based upon their observations.

ICT was also used to support children when interpreting their findings. Children were asked to explain *why* one material was a better thermal insulator than another.

At this point in the lesson, children had the opportunity to look at different materials under a digital microscope (Easi-Scope) so that they could begin to appreciate that the arrangement of fibres influenced how good a material is at keeping the ice cold. Photographs were taken of the different types of material to enable children to use evidence to explain their findings (see Figure 5.3). Without the use of ICT in this lesson, it might have been more difficult for children to compare the materials and to make a reasoned explanation as to which is the best type of thermal insulator and why. In order to develop children's scientific language, a visualiser was used to draw attention to the arrangement of fibres and to help children to understand that the long fibres help to trap the air, making the furry fabrics better thermal insulators.

Figure 5.3   Communicating findings using ICT

Dear Gru,

I am writing to tell you which is the best material to use to keep the ice frozen. We wrapped ice in different types of materials and observed to see which one stopped the ice from melting. The furry materials were best. You might like to think about wearing a furry coat so that you can throw it over the ice and keep it frozen. Here is a picture of the best material. I used a digital microscope and you can see that there are lots of long fibres that trap the air. The air is a good thermal insulator.

I hope this helps.

Best wishes,

Daniel

The purple and brown material kept the ice frozen for the longest because air was trapped in the material. The grey and green were the worst because they are thin (you can see through them).

Children were provided with a choice over how they presented their findings. Some chose to type a sentence; another group of children worked with a TA and together they used a floor book to record their findings, and a third group of children decided to write a letter back to Gru to explain their findings (see Figure 5.3). The use of ICT in this instance enabled oral communication skills to be developed. Children were encouraged to consider the correct use of scientific language such as 'thermal insulator' and to use the word 'material' correctly.

Variations to try

Clicker software is designed to support the development of children's literacy skills and use of scientific language. It can be used across all abilities, and it can also support children who use eyegaze to access personalised literacy support. Word banks can be produced by the teacher in advance of the lesson in order to support the development of scientific vocabulary.

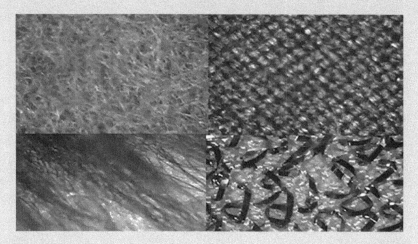

Figure 5.4   Different materials

Speech to text programmes such as Dragon NaturallySpeaking or Siri can also support the recording of children's findings. Such software can be useful for children who have slow writing speeds, as it allows them to be fully included in group reporting activities such as the letter writing illustrated in this case study.

It is important that you are up to date with children's interests so that you can modify your starter according to films and books that are engaging to children at the time.

Reflective question

- The teacher collected evidence in a written format. Is this the best way to assess and capture the thinking behind the science concepts? You might like to consider whether other assessment methods would allow us to understand children's thinking.

Case study 2: Identifying natural specimens

This lesson was delivered to a class of Year 1 children with moderate and complex learning difficulties, towards the beginning of a unit of work. To stimulate curiosity, children were read *The Lorax* by Dr Seuss and were presented with the problem that the Lorax (who speaks for the trees) has muddled up his pictures and names of different trees and cannot remember their names. It is important that the Lorax knows the names of the trees so that he can care for them. Children were asked to help the Lorax by identifying different common trees in the school grounds. They were then asked to think about how they could share this information with the Lorax.

To engage children in naming different trees, they were taken outside the classroom to where a QR trail was set up in a wooded area of the school grounds (see Figure 5.5). QR codes (**Q**uick **R**esponse codes) are a type of two-dimensional barcode that can be read using smartphones and dedicated *QR* reading devices that link directly to text, emails, websites, phone numbers, etc. This format of trail was chosen for the children to follow as it gave them access to information that they could discover independently. The QR codes in this case study had been generated by the teacher using the website www.qrstuff.com. Children used the i-pads to identify the names of the trees included in the QR tree trail, but also used the camera and video feature on the tablets in order to support learning back in the classroom and to make the process of recording memorable. Children were also required to use their senses, so some took wax crayon rubbings of the bark and leaves, while others were encouraged to smell the leaves and bark.

Back in the classroom, children were asked to use ICT to help the Lorax relearn the names of the different trees found in the school grounds. A range of media could have been employed to help children to present their ideas. In this lesson children used i-movies because it enabled them to combine video clips, audio soundbites and

Figure 5.5 How the QR code was set up

pictures. The use of the iPads helped to develop verbal communication skills while at the same time developing understanding of science concepts. It was found that the use of ICT provided children with the opportunity of producing a stimulating presentation regardless of their literacy skills. Children were also provided with the opportunity to evaluate each other's work and use scientific vocabulary (trunk, leaves, fruit, branches, seeds) when comparing and describing different trees.

Variations to try

A range of other media sources may be used to support children's communication skills including:

- Photo Story is a free resource that allows children to drag and arrange photographs and add a narration. The photographs are then merged into a slide show.

- Prezi is a free alternative to PowerPoint.

- PicCollage allows children to produce collages using pictures and texts and can be shared on Facebook, Twitter, Instagram or emailed as a physical postcard.

Children with visual impairment may prefer the QR codes to be printed on cream or buff-coloured paper. If the QR code is generated to lead to text, the size of font should be considered. Many children prefer that the font size should be 12-point or larger.

Stories are a good starting point to engage children and to present a problem or question for them to solve. *Storyboard Science* (Blair, 2011) provides a useful starting point to problem posing. Other useful lesson starters can be found in *Spellbound Science* by Keogh and Naylor (2007).

When children are working in an environment, a useful alternative to QR codes may be the use of a software package called Aurasma. This uses an image which is overlayed with media in the form of animations or videos.

Reflective question

- A student teacher decided to take the children out of the classroom to look for minibeasts that live on or near an oak tree. iPads were taken outside so that children could use the internet to research the names of the minibeasts observed rather than using printed identification guides. Is this a good use of ICT? Remember, at its best ICT should do something that cannot be achieved otherwise, or enable it to be achieved more effectively.

Case study 3: Electrical circuits

A Year 6 class of pupils with moderate learning difficulties undertook a unit of work on electricity and constructed simple circuits to explore what happens when different components are added to the circuit. The children were introduced to circuit symbols

Figure 5.6   The circuit and card design

and practised using these when recording their circuit diagrams. As part of the unit of work, children played computer games to help consolidate their learning. Due to the interactive nature of the games, children were presented with the opportunity for repeated problem solving and appeared motivated to play the games.

The teacher wanted to provide children with the opportunity to apply their learning and practise the skills they had been taught. As the Summer Fayre was fast approaching, she thought she would encourage children to make cards that could be sold. She had found a website (www.lightstitches.co.uk/chibitronics) that sold circuit pieces that could be peeled and stuck on to card to make a simple circuit. With the addition of LED lights, the children were able to make cards that lit up. Children were provided with a simple circuit template in order to practise making the circuit using the circuit pieces. After this, they were required to draw their own circuit using circuit symbols that were then photocopied so that others could use the template to make cards. This provided the opportunity for communication skills to be developed as children were able to provide feedback to their peers about the success of the circuit. The use of the circuit stickers also supported children who had poor fine motor skills as they were able to make a circuit without having to use clips and wires.

Variation

The stick on circuits could be used in a number of other ways. It is possible to add switches to the simple circuit and children could be asked to make a burglar alarm.

Discussion

Pedagogy underpinning the case studies

Humans are innately curious and school science should aim to cultivate this curiosity because 'curious learners' are inclined to want to make sense of their world. Stimulating curiosity begins by teaching children to observe systematically because careful observations of an interesting artefact or event should stimulate thought and questions. However, children need to be interested or have a reason to observe and question the world around them, so teachers need to plan their lessons with this in mind. The decisions a teacher makes about how a concept is introduced and the planned practical activities play a crucial role in determining how children will participate during lessons.

The importance of children actively constructing their knowledge through practical experiences and discussion is recognised across the world as being an effective way for children to learn science (Duggan and Gott, 2002; Kim and Tan, 2011; Sharp et al., 2011). Indeed, Posner et al. (1982) argue that learning is a type of enquiry and the learner often evaluates their understanding based on the evidence presented by investigative work. In enquiry-based lessons children should have the opportunity to organise their evidence and ideas in order to communicate *how* and *why* something happens (Duschl et al., 2006). The key word referred to throughout this chapter is 'communication' and in each of the case studies presented, children used ICT to help them to communicate their understanding of both science skills and concepts. The use of iMovie, digital microscopes and Talking Tins enabled children to organise their thinking in order to demonstrate an understanding of the data collected from their enquiries.

The relationship between science, technology and the outdoor environment aided children's understanding of tree types in Case Study 2. The use of technology enthused and motivated children to find out information about trees using a QR trail. However, it was also important that children used all their senses to appreciate the similarities and differences between the trees (including the smell and feel of the bark and leaves). The lesson could have been conducted remotely in the classroom by viewing websites or DVD/CDs but being outside provided first-hand, memorable experiences that could be developed back in the classroom. Indeed, Waite (2007, p. 335) argues that *positive emotions contribute to enduring memories* when working outside, and these were captured and communicated through ICT when children were working in the classroom.

From a Vygotskian perspective, learning through hands-on learning experiences facilitates children's understanding of science concepts because they are actively engaged and challenged using problem solving which requires them to talk and question ideas. In each case study, children were able to engage in a type of enquiry (fair testing or classifying and sorting) to help either Gru or the Lorax to resolve a problem. A story was presented to the children in Case Study 2 because research suggests that using a story as a stimulus aids concentration, stimulates thinking and provides an effective stimulus for learning (Cavendish et al., 2006). However, it was important to find a story that linked to the outcomes of the lesson so that progression in learning could be secured. The stories generated involvement as children could see a clear purpose to the learning and wanted to help the Lorax to identify the trees.

Enquiries that stem from stories and problems can be perceived as a question-driven learning process whereby children investigate a problem, look for evidence, explain and evaluate their work before finally returning to the original question (Kawalkar and Vijapurkar, 2013). However, Engle and Conant (2002) maintain that children need to have time to interact and talk with their peers and teachers because, as the enquiry unfolds, so discourse and questions emerge. Vygotsky (1978) identified that higher order thinking happens first in a social plane through social interactions and talk, and later in an intrapersonal plane (inside the learner's head). This highlights the importance of collaboration between the child and the teacher (or another child) and the value of dialogue while negotiating the zone of proximal development: the zone between what a learner can do or understand without assistance and what they can do with assistance. The 'assistance' could be in the form of feedback, modelling of ideas, explaining, questioning or task structuring, and the support may be provided by teachers and/or peers (Newton and Newton, 2001). Talk makes it possible for children to assess what they know and offers the chance for them to modify their thinking (Barnes, 2008).

The value of talk in the process of learning is well established, with researchers such as Mercer (2010) drawing on the sociocultural construction of knowledge. According to sociocultural theory, ideas and explanations are co-constructed during classroom and group discussions, and the way in which the teacher orchestrates opportunities for talk is key if learning is to be successful (Vygotsky, 1978; Mercer, 2010). Indeed, Hackling et al. (2011) argue that exploratory forms of talk in which tentative ideas are presented and discussed for evaluation and refinement are valuable for developing understanding.

Concept cartons are designed to stimulate talk using Vygotskian principles and enable children to construct their understanding by presenting them with a problem or challenge (Simon et al., 2008), as identified in the first case study. They are particularly effective if the problem is within the child's grasp but in advance of their reasoning because children are more likely to talk about how the problem can be solved. In order to provide 'challenge', children should work in the zone of proximal development (Vygotsky, 1978). Talk is conducive to learning in this model because talking helps children to clarify their thinking and develops their reasoning skills as well as developing their scientific vocabulary.

Assessment

It can be difficult to find out what children with complex learning difficulties know and understand in relation to their skills in scientific enquiry. Where recorded learning may not be an accurate reflection of their cognitive ability, it is important to consider alternative methods of assessment. Teachers need to understand what all their pupils know and can do in order to plan and implement further learning. The reliance of written forms of evidence for assessment may lead to the key scientific skill of the learner being overlooked.

The Engagement Profile and Scale is a classroom assessment tool developed through SSAT (The School, Student and Teachers network) research into effective teaching and learning for children with complex learning difficulties and disabilities. It allows teachers to focus on the child's engagement with the curriculum as a learner and create personalised learning pathways. It prompts student-centred reflection on how to increase the learner's engagement, leading to deep learning.

An alternative to the Engagement Profile is Learning Tracks, produced by Furby and Catlow (2016). Learning Tracks is an online, printable planning and tracking booklet written to support the planning and assessment of learning for children and young people with severe and complex learning difficulties. The framework of this assessment tool is based on an extended Bloom's Taxonomy (Bloom et al., 1956).

Summary and Key Points

The case studies outlined in this chapter highlight how science and ICT can be used to provide access to children's learning of process skills and concepts in science. Regardless of the learning barriers that are faced, the case studies demonstrate how ICT can be used to engage children in the learning opportunities while developing their self-esteem through activities they can access with levels of independence. This chapter specifically focuses on how ICT can be employed to develop children's skills of communication and collaboration. ICT as a tool enables learners to be free to experiment and explore when working scientifically and highlights the thinking that underlies it. This will help them to construct their own understanding of the topic, assisted by suitable scaffolding from the teacher. However, teachers need to be cognisant that using ICT should enable learners to meet the learning intentions of the lesson. The use of ICT should 'do something' that cannot be achieved without its use or enable learning to be achieved more effectively. For example, it would be an ineffective use of ICT if children were required to research minibeasts using search engines rather than making reference to identification keys when working outside the classroom. Children would probably waste time trying to find suitable websites. Conversely, the use of ICT to help children to communicate effectively would be a good use of ICT because it enables children with literacy difficulties to show their true cognitive ability. The use of oral recorders and video provides children with the time to process the information they have collected when undertaking a science investigation; they are able to revisit their thoughts and ideas when considering evidence and drawing conclusions. This mitigates against time being lost due to the potential anxiety levels becoming a barrier when children are required to record their findings in a written format.

Useful links and further reading

Furby, L and Catlow, J (2016) *Learning Tracks: Planning and Assessing Learning for Children with Severe and Complex Needs*. London: Sage. (Online, printable planning and tracking booklet written to support the planning and assessment needs of learning.)

www.qrstuff.com: a website to generate QR codes.

www.talkingpoint.org.uk/teachers/helping-children-access-curriculum: tips for helping children to access the curriculum.

www.thecommunicationtrust.org.uk/media/21024/ways_of_recording.pdf: alternative methods to written recording.

References

Barnes, D with Mercer, B and Hodginson, S (eds) (2008) *Exploratory Talk for Learning in Exploring Talk in School*. London: Sage.

Blair, G (2011) *Storyboard Science. Wolverhampton:* Learning Materials. Available at: www. Learningmaterials. co.uk/Secondary/Storyboard-Science (accessed 22 August 2017).

Cavendish, J, Stopps B and Ryan, C (2006) Involving young children through stories as starting points. *Primary Science Review*, 92, 18–20.

Department for Education (DfE) (2015) *Special Educational Needs and Disability Code of Practice: 0 to 25 years. Statutory guidance for organisations which work with and support children and young people who have special educational needs or disabilities.* Available at: www.gov.uk/government/uploads/system/uploads/attachment_data/file/398815/SEND_Code_of_Practice_January_2015.pdf (accessed 22 August 2017).

Department for Education (DfE) (2011) *Teachers' Standards.* Available at: www.gov.uk/government/uploads/system/uploads/attachment_data/file/283566/Teachers_standard_information.pdf (accessed 22 August 2017).

Department for Education (DfE) (2013) *National Curriculum in England: Science Programme of Study.* Available at: www.gov.uk/government/uploads/system/uploads/attachment_data/file/425618/PRIMARY_national_curriculum_-_Science.pdf (accessed 22 August 2017).

Duggan, S and Gott, R (2002) What sort of science education do we really need? *International Journal of Science Education*, 24(7): 661–79.

Duschl, RA, Schweingruber, HA and House, AW (eds) (2006) *Taking Science to School: Learning and Teaching Science in Grades K-8.* Washington, DC: The National Academies Press.

Dyson, A (1990) Special educational needs and the concept of change. *Oxford Review of Education,* 16(1): 55–66.

Engle, RA and Conant, FR (2002) Guiding principles for fostering productive disciplinary engagement: Explaining an emergent argument in a community of learner's classroom. *Cognition and Instruction*, 20(4): 34–83.

Furby, L and Catlow, J (2016) *Learning Tracks: Planning and Assessing Learning for Children with Severe and Complex Needs.* London: Sage.

Hacking, M, Smith, P and Murcia, K (2011) Enhancing classroom discourse in primary science: The Puppets Project. *Teaching Science,* 57(2): 18–25.

Kawalkar, A and Vijapurkar, J (2013) Scaffolding science talk: The role of teachers' questions in the inquiry classroom. *International Journal of Science Education*, 35(12): 2004–27.

Keogh, B and Naylor, S (2007) *Spellbound Science.* Sandbach: Millgate Publishing.

Kim, M and Tan, A (2011) Rethinking difficulties of teaching inquiry-based practical work: Stories from elementary pre-service teaches. *International Journal of Science Education*, 33(4): 465–86.

Mercer, N (2010) The analysis of classroom talk: Methods and methodologies. *British Journal of Educational Psychology*, 80: 1–14.

Naylor, S and Keogh, B (2000) *Concept Cartoons in Science Education.* Sandbach: Millgate Publishers.

Newton, DP and Newton, LD (2001) Subject content knowledge and teacher talk in the primary science classroom. *European Journal of Teacher Education*, 24(3): 369–401.

Posner GJ, Strike, KA, Hewson, PW and Gertzog, WA (1982) Accommodation of a scientific conception: Towards a theory of conceptual change. *Science Education*, 66(2): 211–27.

Sharp, JG, Hopkin, R and Lewthwaite, B (2011) Teacher perceptions of science in the National Curriculum: Findings from an application of the Science Curriculum Implementation Questionnaire in English primary schools. *International Journal of Science Education*, 33(17): 2407–36.

Simon, S, Stuart, N, Keogh, B, Maloney, J and Downing, B (2008) Puppets promoting engagement and talk in science, *International Journal of Science Education,* 30(9): 1129–48.

Vygotsky, LS (1978) *Mind in Society: The Development of Higher Psychological Processes.* Cambridge, MA: Harvard University Press.

Waite, S (2007) Memories are made of this: Some reflections on outdoor learning and recall. *Education, 3–13,* 35(4): 333–47.

Chapter 6

DESIGN AND TECHNOLOGY

KIM AVERY AND STEVE CULLINGFORD-AGNEW

Introduction

This chapter focuses on how Information Communication Technology (ICT) can enhance children's learning in Design and Technology. This is a subject which is very practical and allows pupils to reach a given outcome through trial and error, a fundamental aspect of computational thinking. During Design and Technology lessons, teachers need to encourage pupils to take risks with their thinking and be creative.

Pupils should be guided to:

- develop the creative, technical and practical expertise needed to perform everyday tasks confidently and to participate successfully in an increasingly technological world;

- build and apply a repertoire of knowledge, understanding and skills in order to design and make high-quality prototypes and products for a wide range of users;

- critique, evaluate and test their ideas and products and the work of others.

(DfE, 2013)

This chapter will give guidance on how to use technology in the classroom to support creativity for all pupils. It will give suggestions of software available to support in the prototype and product stages of making, as well as addressing means to make effective evaluations of completed projects. This chapter will also look at technologies that have been developed to support pupils with SEND and help to ensure that they gain full access to the curriculum, and how to effectively assess within design and technology.

Learning objectives

At the end of this chapter you should be able to:

- reflect upon a range of software available to support creativity within the design and making process;
- identify ways in which communication and collaborative working are key to expanding pupils' creativity and idea making;
- identify ways in which technology can be used to support the teaching of design and technology.

Links to Teachers' Standards

1. **set high expectations which inspire, motivate and challenge pupils**

   - establish a safe and stimulating environment for pupils, rooted in mutual respect;
   - set goals that stretch and challenge pupils of all backgrounds, abilities and dispositions.

2. **Promote good progress and outcomes by pupils**

   - be accountable for pupils' attainment, progress and outcomes;
   - be aware of pupils' capabilities and their prior knowledge, and plan teaching to build on these;
   - guide pupils to reflect on the progress they have made and their emerging needs;
   - demonstrate knowledge and understanding of how pupils learn and how this impacts on teaching;
   - encourage pupils to take a responsible and conscientious attitude to their own work and study.

3. **Demonstrate good subject and curriculum knowledge**

   - have a secure knowledge of the relevant subject(s) and curriculum areas, foster and maintain pupils' interest in the subject, and address misunderstandings;
   - demonstrate a critical understanding of developments in the subject and curriculum areas, and promote the value of scholarship.

5. **Adapt teaching to respond to the strengths and needs of all pupils**

   - know when and how to differentiate appropriately, using approaches which enable pupils to be taught effectively;
   - have a secure understanding of how a range of factors can inhibit pupils' ability to learn, and how best to overcome these;
   - demonstrate an awareness of the physical, social and intellectual development of children, and know how to adapt teaching to support pupils' education at different stages of development;
   - have a clear understanding of the needs of all pupils, including those with special educational needs; those of high ability; those with English as an additional language; those with disabilities; and be able to use and evaluate distinctive teaching approaches to engage and support them.

6. **Make accurate and productive use of assessment**

   - give pupils regular feedback, both orally and through accurate marking, and encourage pupils to respond to the feedback.

Links to National Curriculum Programmmes of Study: Design and Technology

Key Stage 1 and 2

Through a variety of creative and practical activities, pupils should be taught the knowledge, understanding and skills needed to engage in an iterative process of designing and making. They should work in a range of relevant contexts – for example, the home and school, gardens and playgrounds, the local community, industry and the wider environment.

When designing and making, pupils should be taught to:

Key Stage 1

Design

- generate, develop, model and communicate their ideas through talking, drawing, templates, mock-ups and, where appropriate, information and communication technology;

Evaluate

- evaluate their ideas and products against design criteria;

Technical knowledge

- explore and use mechanisms – for example, levers, sliders, wheels and axles – in their products.

Key Stage 2

Design

- use research and develop design criteria to inform the design of innovative, functional, appealing products that are fit for purpose, aimed at particular individuals or groups;
- generate, develop, model and communicate their ideas through discussion, annotated sketches, cross-sectional and exploded diagrams, prototypes, pattern pieces and computer-aided design.

Make

- select from and use a wider range of materials and components, including construction materials, textiles and ingredients, according to their functional properties and aesthetic qualities.

Evaluate

- investigate and analyse a range of existing products;
- evaluate their ideas and products against their own design criteria and consider the views of others to improve their work.

Technical knowledge

- understand and use mechanical systems in their products – for example, gears, pulleys, cams, levers and linkages;
- understand and use electrical systems in their products – for example, series circuits incorporating switches, bulbs, buzzers and motors;
- apply their understanding of computing to program, monitor and control their products.

Case study 1: Lego WeDo

When introducing a design and technology theme, the purpose of the product should be paramount to the designer, in this case the children. Lego WeDo is a tool that can encourage children to be inventive with technology. In this case study we will look at using it to create a new toy.

Pupil learning outcomes

- To plan and create a new toy.

- To create a toy for a given audience.

- To program a sequence of movement.

- To debug and improve the programing of a toy.

Technologies used

This case study uses the Lego WeDo kit. However, the motors can be bought independently of the kit boxes and would be a cheaper alternative if your school already has access to Lego. To create the storyboards, Lego have a free storyboarding app, StoryVisualizer, where you can create storyboards, adding images, text and comic features to support the ideas stage.

Impact on learning

When introducing this project, it is important to initially look at the robotics aspect and give pupils time to explore the Lego WeDo resources. There are a number of pre-designed characters you can make as a starting point. Ensure that pupils understand how to use the software to program their characters before moving on to creating stories.

Once the children have these skills, it is time to move on to look at the design criteria. An interesting way of doing this is to create a Dragons' Den theme, and you may like to present the class with a video of a presenter sharing their challenge to create a new toy for a company. Ensure that pupils are aware of the design criteria, such as the age of children the toy is aimed at.

There are many apps that can support pupils with their ideas. ScratchJnr (www.scratchjr. org) is a free app which pupils could use to design their toy prototypes and program them to move or talk. It is a simplified version of Scratch which may be apt for pupils with SEND. It is easier to follow and can be used on an iPad or a tablet which may help pupils who struggle with fine motor skills. Pupils could make a number of prototypes and decide their favourite individually or through the use of peer assessment.

Once the toy designs have been decided, pupils can create their characters using the Lego WeDo kits. This can be done individually or you may want to set the class the

Figure 6.1   Toy design using LegoWedo kits

Figure 6.2   Toy design using LegoWedo kits

challenge of working collaboratively. Building items such as these provides a context for developing children's communication and negotiation skills. Think carefully about what you will set your SEND pupils to achieve; it may well be a challenge enough to decide on one of the pre-made characters and follow the steps to make this for their toy.

Figure 6.3 Presentations by Little Story Creator

When the toys are complete with their moving parts, it is important to look back at the design criteria and think about how pupils are going to present their ideas to the 'Dragons'. Allow pupils time to create a presentation, which itself could be presented using a variety of ways. Little Story Creator can be a useful app for pupils with cognitive disabilities, as it offers a simplified means to insert images, add text and then manipulate them on the presentation pages.

When presenting ideas at the end of the project, encourage pupils to question each other's design ideas and to be self-reflective. An important question here would be, 'What would you do to make it better next time?'

Variations to try

- When making your prototypes you could use alternative software to ScratchJnr. You could consider using the StoryVisualizer app, which allows pupils to write text alongside images. You might find some inspiring ideas for Lego WeDo at Dr E's WeDo Challenges, available at: wedo.dreschallenges.com.

- If you don't need to make the physical item, this work could be completed on screen as a prototype project. This would allow you to use programing tools such as Scratch to create and program the toys.

- When presenting your ideas, you could use PowerPoint or a tablet. Alternative presentation apps are KeyNote and EverNote, both of which work in much the same way.

Case study 2: Makey Makey

There are numerous ways in which you can use Makey Makey kits which allow pupils to explore using their curiosity, many of which involve music and can be found on their site, http://makeymakey.com/gallery. However, I found the game controller element of Makey Makey to be particularly interesting to pupils. This allows pupils to create a game and use a different means of access.

Pupil learning outcomes

- To plan and create a game.
- To create a game for a given audience.
- To create a game pad.
- To test and evaluate a game.

Technologies used

This case study looks at the Makey Makey kit and how this can support the design and technology curriculum. The kit can be used with the Scratch program and allows for exploration of creative programming.

Impact on learning

This activity could be introduced as the task of designing a new game for one of the leading games console companies. Give the pupils a brief of what they need to produce. Take into account the type of game you want them to produce and any themes you may want them to adhere to. Within this you need to highlight that a design feature you are looking at is the game controller.

As part of the technical knowledge aspect of design and technology, pupils could spend some time researching the design of existing controllers and ask other pupils what they like or dislike about them. This should help them design something that will capture their audience's attention. As with all design and technology projects, the process should focus attention on trial and error in design.

When designing their game, pupils will need time to plan the ideas first. This could be done in a similar manner to the previous example using Little Story Creator, which is a simple means to insert images, add text and manipulate them on the presentation pages. Pupils can take photographs of their hand drawn designs and add comments around the images.

During the make phase pupils will need to pay particular attention to the making of the controller: What materials will be used? How will the controller be activated? What design will the control have? These are important factors to consider when creating the product and thinking about how the audience will receive it. Encouraging pupils to experiment with their ideas can be a really creative process. Once the games are completed, allow pupils to evaluate their work and peer assess them. Makey Makey can be a useful hands-on resource for demonstrating cause and effect outcomes for pupils with SEND. It could be adapted to support a range of needs and the objects used alongside the kit altered depending on pupils' dexterity. For example, a larger object could be used for those who struggle with fine motor skills.

Variations to try

- You could create the game and controller using a Raspberry Pi and Micro:bit together (see www.raspberrypi.org/learning/microbit-game-controller). This would work in the same way but may stretch your more able pupils with their computing knowledge.

- When making your plans, you could use the Story Visualizer app from Lego, which allows pupils to take images and write text alongside it.

- A range of examples of how to use the Makey Makey kits can be found on their site at: www.makeymakey.com.

- Find out more about makerspaces and accessible resources at: https://jenmadeit.com

Case study 3: Music technology

There are several software options you can use for inclusive and creative music-making. This case study focuses on thematic composition, such as to recreate a rainforest or ocean environment.

Pupil learning outcomes

- To identify sounds in a given environment.
- To use software to re-create sounds.
- To create a piece of music.
- To evaluate a piece of music.

Technologies used

This case study looks at Incredibox, which is a fantastic free website where you can create and save your own music, available at: www.incredibox.com. The site has four versions of the program and each has a range of sounds including beats, effects, melodies and voice samples which the player can select to build up their piece of music.

Impact on learning

Music technology can be used for a wide range of technology projects. This case study will demonstrate how you could use technology to create a rainforest environment. When introducing a new theme, it is important to ensure that children's prior learning is taken into account.

Expose the pupils to the rainforest theme through a range of resources that cater to all learners. For example:

- Create a sensory environment, perhaps in a muddy or marshy area, in which pupils can touch different types of leaves and vegetation. They could also explore the foods found in the rainforest.

- Listen to the sounds of the rainforest, the vegetation, animals and weather. Discuss with pupils how they may be able to recreate these sounds. Are there musical instruments they could use?

- Look at images of the rainforest and encourage pupils to discuss what they can see and how these might influence their choices when creating a piece of music to fit the theme.

Once you have introduced the theme, give pupils time to discuss and trial ideas for different sounds. This is where you can introduce the Incredibox software and allow pupils to start to build pieces of music and test them on a given audience. As music can be very emotive, there are links to emotions which you could draw upon. How does the music make them feel? What atmosphere does it create? Once their music is completed, you could set up the sensory environment again and invite an audience (possibly other classes) to experience the environment with the pupils' music playing. Remember the importance of evaluating work, taking into account the audience response.

Variations to try

- There are a number of online music creator programs such as www.isleoftune.com, or apps such as GarageBand and MadPad which capture environmental sounds to create music.

- Alternative themes for a music technology project could be to create a piece of music for a given establishment such as a coffee shop. This may need a visit to the site to understand the type of music needed.

- You could also create a piece of music for a genre of music such as hip hop, pop music or rock.

Discussion

Developing, planning and communicating ideas are fundamental themes within design and technology, and ICT offers a range of tools to support these skills, as described by BECTA:

In the same way that ICT has revolutionised the design and manufacturing processes in the industrial and commercial world, ICT can help pupils' learning in design and technology, by:

- *enhancing their capability to explore and develop their ideas;*

- *enhancing their ability to communicate and present their ideas;*

- *providing a range of information sources to enhance their design and technology knowledge;*

- *providing an increased range of tools, equipment, materials and components for their products.*

Becta (2009) ICT in Design and Technology (D&T): A pupil's entitlement (p.2)

For example: construction involves children developing the skills to use various ICT tools to design, join and combine materials for a purpose; evaluating involves aspects of collaboration in which children are encouraged to evaluate their own designs as well as those of others. This encourages them to reflect on their work, suggesting ways in which it could be improved or further developed.

Developing, planning and communicating can be supported using media, video, photographs, recording, symbols and literacy software. To refer to the literacy chapter, Clicker 7 and Inprint 3 offer excellent resources to support pictorial ways of sequencing, following instructions, planning ideas, making designs and evaluating work. For example, children can use symbols, photographs and digital writing frames to aid access and understanding of concepts across subjects. This draws upon the Universal Design for Learning (UDL) approach that facilitates different types of access using different media channels to aid expression (see Chapter 2).

For some children with SEND the use of technology can help overcome access issues. It might be that they do not have the fine motor skills to undertake a task or have a sensory impairment. Technology can be used to modify access and thus make a range of additional learning tools available. This is noted by Davies (2004) who states that:

One of the benefits of using ICT is that the quality of the product can be greatly enhanced as the pupils are not limited by their motor skills or held back by their difficulties in presenting their ideas in design, drawing, or have to rely on the teacher for oral instructions. (p.67)

We might go on to evaluate our use of technology in the light of Bloom's Taxonomy to ask what the technology adds to the student's learning, and whether it promotes higher forms of thinking, such as analysing and evaluating concepts, processes, procedures, and principles. Bloom's Taxonomy can also be a useful framework for designing tasks, planning questions and providing feedback.

- **Knowledge**: Recall of facts, terms and concepts. Who? What? Where? When? How?

- **Comprehension**: The ability to understand the meaning, basic interpretation, or an ability to summarise. What do we mean by? Can you explain?

- **Application**: The ability to use learned materials in new concrete situations. What other examples are there?

- **Analysis**: The ability to break down materials into component parts so that the structure may be understood. What is the evidence for parts or features of?

- **Synthesis**: The ability to put parts together to form a new whole. How could we add to? Improve? Design? Solve?

- **Evaluation**: The ability to make judgements about the value of learned materials, particularly in relation to a given context or need. What do you think about? What are the assessment criteria?

We can use this framework to help us aim for high expectations as a fundamental principle in all our teaching and we can encourage children to use technology to produce high quality digital artefacts representing their learning. As Davies (2004) suggests:

> *Pupils with SEN should have high expectations; they are surrounded by high quality images and products and become highly motivated when they realise that using ICT means that they can produce 'professional' looking designs and products.* (p.67)

ICT can also be used to involve pupils in peer and self-assessment, and to share what they have learnt and created. See Chapter 9 for more ideas on assessment.

Food Technology

Food technology has always been an important aspect of learning in terms of life skills and independent living, as well as offering children and young people a range of sensory experiences. The statement within the QCA Design and Technology document (2009) notes that:

> *Design and technology (D&T) provides practical learning experiences which make it accessible to all pupils. Pupils use knowledge and understanding from across the curriculum and apply and consolidate them in practical activities. Designing and making real products that can be used can give pupils a sense of achievement and improve their self-esteem. They benefit from seeing their own progress and taking greater responsibility for their own learning as they begin to evaluate the quality of their work. Pupils' personal involvement with tasks often improves their attention span, patience, persistence and commitment.* (p.4)

There are a range of skills involved in food technology that can be supported by ICT. These include sequencing and following instructions, and key skills such as working with others in a team, reflecting on learning, problem solving and independent enquiry. Such skills need to be fostered at an early age for all children, including those with SEND. The key skills can be found in the QCA (2009) 'Developing skills' booklet, and are a really useful way of helping to develop the design and technology framework within a school.

When completing food and technology tasks it is useful to think about breaking down the task into smaller steps and using additional visual supports to ensure those with SEND can understand the expectations. For example, the Shopping List Activity on the Barefoot Computing site (http://barefootcas.org.uk/activities/sen/cake-shopping-list-activity) gives pupils additional structure to allow them to follow the task as independently as they can. A second design and technology activity on the Barefoot Computing site focuses on pupils developing the thinking skill of pattern recognition by identifying similarities between houses and using them to create their own house. Teachers are provided with ways of differentiating the activity according to their pupils' needs, including introducing simple sorting activities for those requiring more support and ideas for extension into Scratch for those working at higher levels. There are also ideas for adaption for pupils with visual and audio impairment: http://barefootcas.org.uk/activities/sen/house-patterns-activity/.

In addition, there are a range of technologies that can improve access to food technology for children with SEND, and a variety of applications to support access to everyday equipment such as microwaves, food mixers, and blenders. An example is the Inclusive Click-On 2 controller (http://www.inclusive.co.uk/inclusive-click-on-2) which can operate two mains devices simultaneously. Devices can then be linked to a range of different switches and, with careful assessment and positioning, can greatly improve access for some children with physical difficulties. An excellent starting point for teaching children how to use switches is the Switch Progression Road Map from Inclusive Technology (http://www.inclusive.co.uk/articles/switch-progression-road-map).

There is also software available to support food technology, such as the virtual kitchen, 'Choose and Cook', from Inclusive Technology (http://www.inclusive.co.uk/choose-and-cook-p22760). This software takes students through the cooking and preparation process. It enables students to practise the skills necessary to plan a healthy meal, select and use the tools and materials they will need for the various processes, and communicate their understanding of what they have learnt through choice-making. Although real experience is important, Choose and Cook enables your class to focus on the processes without being distracted by the physical and cognitive challenges of the practical tasks. This program can be used in tandem with real cooking and home management lessons, as the simple recipes in the program can all be easily produced in the kitchen.

Reflective questions:

- How can design and technology integrate the physical and digital experiences?

- How can technology be used to provide children with access and control?

- How can technology provide communication opportunities to support children in designing, planning, and evaluating their work in collaboration with others?

Summary and Key Points

Design and Technology can provide inclusive opportunities for all children and facilitate cross-curricular skills. The use of ICT in Design and Technology can help children to create high-quality outputs that make links between physical and digital environments, developing their understanding of the real world. The importance of using technology to ensure that we have high expectations of our learners and to offer ways for children to share outcomes and reflect upon their own learning is a key feature within Design and Technology. Technology can offer them opportunities to experience achievement and reflect upon it and, as a result, develop their confidence and self-esteem, both within the subject and across their daily lives.

Further reading

Echeveste, ME (2016) Challenges of introducing Computer Science into the traditional grammar of K-12 schooling, *Proceedings of the 2016 ACM Conference on Innovation and Technology in Computer Science Education*, pp. 359–9.

Ladner, RE and Israel, M (2016) 'For All' in 'Computer Science for All'. *Communications of the ACM*, 59(9): 26–8.

Ludi, S and Reichlmayr, T (2008) Developing inclusive outreach activities for students with visual impairments. SIGCSE '08: *Proceedings of the 39th ACM Technical Symposium on Computer Science Education*, pp. 439–43.

Ludi, S and Reichlmayr, T (2011) The use of robotics to promote computing to pre-college students with visual impairments. *ACM Transactions on Computing Education*, 11(3): 1–20.

Useful links

http://barefootcas.org.uk/activities/sen – aims to support pupils with their computational skills.

http://barefootcas.org.uk/activities/sen/cake-shopping-list-activity – gives pupils additional structure to allow them to follow the task independently.

http://barefootcas.org.uk/activities/sen/house-patterns-activity – supports a Design and Technology project about designing a new house as the activity focuses on finding patterns and what to expect when building a house.

https://jenmadeit.com – website on a makerspace list about someone who is creating accessible resources.

http://makered.org/wp-content/uploads/2014/09/Makerspace-Playbook-Feb-2013.pdf – Maker Movement.

https://wedo.dreschallenges.com – inspiration for Lego WeDo: the activities are varied and inspiring.

www.cricksoft.com/uk/home.aspx – Crick Software.

www.inclusive.co.uk – Inclusive Technology.

www.inclusive.co.uk/articles/switch-progression-road-map – Ian Bean Switch progression map.

www.weareteachers.com/blogs/post/2015/04/03/how-the-maker-movement-is-transforming-education – Maker Movement.

www.widgit.com – Widgit Software.

References

Becta (2009) *ICT in Design and Technology (D&T): A Pupil's Entitlement*. Available at: www.tes.com/teaching-resource/using-ict-in-primary-design-and-technology-6072366 (accessed 27 June 2017).

Bloom, BS (1956) *Taxonomy of Educational Objectives*, Vol. 1. London: Longman.

Davies, L (2005) *Meeting SEN in the Curriculum: Design and Technology*. London: Routledge.

Department for Education (2013) *The National Curriculum in England: design and technology programmes of study*. Available at: https://www.gov.uk/government/publications/national-curriculum-in-england-design-and-technology-programmes-of-study 7 (accessed 24 August 2016).

Qualifications and Curriculum Authority (QCA) (2009a) *Design and Technology: Planning, Teaching and Accessing the Curriculum for Pupils with Learning Difficulties*. Coventry: Qualifications and Curriculum Authority.

QCA (2009b) *Developing Skills: Planning, Teaching and Accessing the Curriculum for Pupils with Learning Difficulties*. Coventry: Qualifications and Curriculum Authority.

Chapter 7

COMPUTING

JOHN GALLOWAY AND SALLY PAVELEY

Introduction

In 1988 the government introduced the first iteration of a National Curriculum, which included the relatively new subject of Information Technology. Over the next twenty-seven years there were a number of tweaks and redesigns, and IT picked up a 'C' (for 'communication') along the way to become ICT, which was taught in schools until 2015, when the latest iteration saw it renamed 'Computing', a deliberate transformation to indicate a shift in emphasis.

Previously, we had strands of 'Finding things out', 'Developing ideas and making things happen', 'Exchanging and sharing information', and 'Reviewing, modifying and evaluating work as it progresses'. Now we have 'digital literacy', 'information technology' and 'computer science'. The content is fairly similar. What has changed is the prominence of coding and programming as core activities where once these had come under the subheading of 'control'. 'ICT' was mainly taught as the skills to achieve in school – research, communication, data analysis, using technology to create and share our ideas. 'Computing' still has those threads, but their importance has diminished in comparison to the need to understand the digital workings of the machines and interfaces around us, how we can take charge of them and harness this knowledge to improve the world in which we live.

Learning objectives

This chapter looks at the National Curriculum requirements for Computing, and in particular the Computer Science element. It considers its place in the education of pupils with special educational needs and disabilities (SEND), and provides case studies to demonstrate practice in both mainstream and specialist provisions.

In this chapter you will learn:

- the relevance and application of the Computing curriculum for pupils with SEND;
- ideas for practical approaches in the classroom, including 'unplugged' activities;
- the range of resources currently available.

Links to Teachers' Standards

S1 **Set high expectations which inspire, motivate and challenge pupils**
Set goals that stretch and challenge pupils of all backgrounds, abilities and dispositions.

S2 **Promote good progress and outcomes by pupils**
Be aware of pupils' capabilities and their prior knowledge, and plan teaching to build on these.

S4 **Plan and teach well-structured lessons**
Impart knowledge and develop understanding through effective use of lesson time.

S5 **Adapt teaching to respond to the strengths and needs of all pupils**
Know when and how to differentiate appropriately, using approaches which enable pupils to be taught effectively.

Have a secure understanding of how a range of factors can inhibit pupils' ability to learn, and how best to overcome these.

Have a clear understanding of the needs of all pupils, including those with special educational needs; those of high ability; those with English as an additional language; those with disabilities; and be able to use and evaluate distinctive teaching approaches to engage and support them.

S7 **Manage behaviour effectively to ensure a good and safe learning environment**
Manage classes effectively, using approaches which are appropriate to pupils' needs in order to involve and motivate them.

Links to National Curriculum Programmes of Study

The case studies presented in this chapter refer to the following content in the National Curriculum:

Key Stage 1 pupils should be taught to:

- understand what algorithms are; how they are implemented as programs on digital devices; and that programs execute by following precise and unambiguous instructions;
- create and debug simple programs;
- use logical reasoning to predict the behaviour of simple programs;
- use technology purposefully to create, organise, store, manipulate and retrieve digital content;
- recognise common uses of information technology beyond school;
- use technology safely and respectfully, keeping personal information private; identify where to go for help and support when they have concerns about content or contact on the internet or other online technologies.

Key Stage 2 pupils should be taught to:

- design, write and debug programs that accomplish specific goals, including controlling or simulating physical systems; solve problems by decomposing them into smaller parts;

- use sequence, selection, and repetition in programs; work with variables and various forms of input and output;
- use logical reasoning to explain how some simple algorithms work and to detect and correct errors in algorithms and programs;
- select, use and combine a variety of software (including internet services) on a range of digital devices to design and create a range of programs, systems and content that accomplish given goals, including collecting, analysing, evaluating and presenting data and information;
- use technology safely, respectfully and responsibly; recognise acceptable/unacceptable behaviour; identify a range of ways to report concerns about content and contact.

The National Curriculum for Computing

The Computing curriculum has three aspects: Computer Science, Information Technology and Digital Literacy. They are explained by Computing at School, the body behind much of the reform.

The core of computing is computer science, in which pupils are taught the principles of information and computation, how digital systems work and how to put this knowledge to use through programming. Building on this knowledge and understanding, pupils are equipped to use information technology to create programs, systems and a range of content. Computing also ensures that pupils become digitally literate – able to use, and express themselves and develop their ideas through, information and communication technology – at a level suitable for the future workplace and as active participants in a digital world.

(Computing at School, 2013)

Most teachers are comfortable with the ideas and concepts of the information technology and digital literacy strands of this revised curriculum. Activities such as searching the internet for information; creating documents and presentations; gathering and interpreting data; making images or taking photos then editing and printing, or sharing, them; using technology to create music; communicating via emails or apps on our phones, and so on – the kinds of activity that are well embedded not only in our classrooms but also in our everyday lives.

For pupils with a range of special educational needs and disabilities, many of these activities will be on the timetable, albeit with varying degrees of challenge and support. Taking a photograph, for instance, is about information technology as learners need an understanding of the device and the process to fulfil the task; they also need to be digitally literate in order to capture the subject successfully and share it with others.

It is Computer Science that causes consternation among teachers, particularly when working with learners with more complex learning difficulties. It is this aspect of the Computing curriculum that this chapter focuses upon.

Case study 1: Engaging a reluctant learner

Jack has autism and was a pupil at The Bridge School. He was cognitively able, working well within the National Curriculum levels with good communication and language skills but he had significant issues with anxiety and self-esteem. When he reached Year 6, Jack refused to come to school. Following a 'team around the child' meeting, James Galpin, a developmental psychologist and member of the school's

Outreach Team, started to make home visits to find out why and to try to motivate Jack to return.

During these visits, Jack's special interest in computers came to the fore and James was able to use this as a way to re-engage Jack in the learning process; he set Jack the challenge of researching the history of computers, then of building his own computer, leaving it to Jack to decide how best to go about this.

> *I was already aware of the Raspberry Pi, but I was hoping the suggestion would come from him. He didn't let me down. 'Have you heard of the Raspberry Pi?' he asked. 'It's a credit-card sized computer and you put it all together yourself and you can see it in action.' 'That sounds brilliant,' I responded. 'Would you like me to see if the school would be willing to buy one? Then perhaps we could go in together and do some work on it.*

> (James Galpin, 2015)

A room was found for Jack at school and this became his 'Pi Workshop'. He returned to school and continued his education in the workshop. He built the Raspberry Pi and quickly learned to code using Python, which was a tremendous boost to his self-esteem. As he stated, 'Programming is just awesome! I've been programming on the Pi from day one.'

It was through learning to code that Jack was able to overcome his intense dislike of getting anything 'wrong'; when he discovered that debugging was a normal part of the coding process he commented, 'It helps you learn that when you make a mistake you can fix it.'

Jack was also able to use the Pi to participate in other subjects. He was aware that his skills in core subjects like handwriting, spelling and maths didn't match his cognitive abilities, so he was reluctant to engage in them. Pi-based projects helped him to overcome this reluctance. For example, he was given the challenge of using logo to create a program that would write his own name and, after he had managed to do this, he commented that 'this is like maths but fun'.

The biggest challenge that was set for Jack was to create a video about the Raspberry Pi. This involved him in planning the story, thinking about what people would find interesting, adding humour, writing a narrative and presenting it in front of a camera. His video is available on Vimeo: http://vimeo.com/95982529.

The differences in cognitive styles some people with autism experience can lead to a greater strength in areas that require a lot of detail-focused processing. Having technology as a special interest is now being recognised by the job market, in particular by technology companies, which presents potential employment opportunities and a brighter future for young people like Jack.

Case study 2: Pupils with complex SEN (SLD/ASC)

The Computer Science element in the Computing curriculum presents a challenge to those teaching pupils who have severe learning difficulties (SLD). These are pupils who are working consistently below National Curriculum expectations with a few perhaps reaching into the early levels of the National Curriculum over time. This latter point is especially relevant for learners with a dual diagnosis of SLD and autism (ASC) who may well be extremely adept at rote learning and appear to 'achieve' but without the necessary understanding (Imray and Colley, 2017). Many of these pupils will be taught in special schools and units.

The challenge is to help pupils who have SLD and/or autism to learn skills that are meaningful and transferable and to equip teachers to provide them with learning experiences that fulfil these criteria. Computer Science is essentially about problem solving in a systematic way by identifying the steps needed to complete a task that will solve a problem, then carrying out the task one step at a time and changing the sequence of the steps if it doesn't work. It could be about carrying out everyday tasks such as making a sandwich if you are hungry, or learning how to control everyday devices and appliances such as using a pelican crossing to cross a road safely, or programming a microwave to make popcorn. It could also be turning your teacher into a robot or a dinosaur and programming her to carry out your instructions, or having fun playing problem-solving computer games, or even starting to write your own code.

Robot Games at The Bridge School

Robot Games was a series of five lessons designed to introduce the concept of giving commands to control (program) a robot to a group of Key Stage 2 pupils who have severe learning difficulties and/or autism. We chose pupils we felt would enjoy the games and understand their purpose. These were pupils who were working at pre-National Curriculum expectations, and into the early National Curriculum levels.

We created a 'Name the Robot' PowerPoint quiz to start the lesson as robots were both familiar and motivating to the pupils. The quiz consisted of photos of robots from popular TV shows and movies and culminated in a photo of their class teacher wearing a robot hat. This PowerPoint was developed further to reinforce the commands in later lessons as some of the pupils found the terms 'backwards' and 'forwards' quite difficult to conceptualise when applied to another person (or robot).

The class teacher designed and made 'robot hats' from empty A4 paper boxes covered with silver foil. She stuck a red (left) and green (right) circle on either side of the hat to help the pupils distinguish between left and right. While we envisaged that staff would play the role of robot the pupils made it clear that they wanted to be robots too.

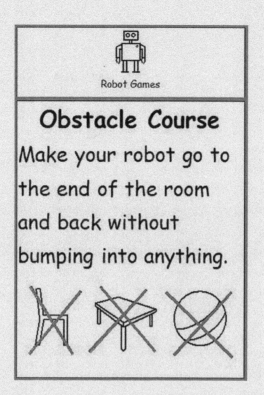

Figure 7.1 Obstacle course

We used SymWriter 2, a desktop publishing program from Widgit Software: www. widgit.com) to create visuals to help pupils to remember the commands.

After the PowerPoint starter, the pupils were asked to send a robot (a member of staff wearing the robot hat) to a place in the room. When the robot didn't respond to random instructions, we explained that the robot only understands certain words. At this point, we introduced the cards showing the command vocabulary and encouraged the pupils to use these. They were also introduced to the concept of using numbers to tell the robot how many steps to take.

All the pupils in the group had a turn at giving commands to the robot, then they split into pairs and took their own 'robots' to do the Robot Challenge. The first challenge was to make the robots complete an obstacle course. It became clear that most of the pupils needed lots of practice with the basic commands, so we continued with this activity in subsequent lessons. However, two of the pupils understood how to control their robot and became adept controllers in the first session. They were able to estimate and add the number of steps needed to their commands to make their robot move more efficiently. These pupils were also very good at problem-solving games involving position and direction on the computer and had well-developed language skills.

The other pupils took longer to engage successfully with the games. Some did not appear to understand that they needed to make the robot carry out a specific task – i.e.

Figure 7.2 Visuals to help remember commands

go to the end of the room – although they were able to make the robot move one step at a time. While one of these pupils was also very good at problem solving computer games involving position and direction, he was non-verbal and had significant difficulties with receptive language. He may not have fully understood what he was being asked to do. Another pupil in this group had good expressive language skills but struggled with games involving position and direction and, while he was able to use the commands, he did so in a fairly random way.

This would suggest that the computational thinking skills required to move beyond the concrete action of using direct instructions to control the robot one step at a time – e.g. 'forward' – to the more abstract notion of thinking ahead to what the robot will need to do in terms of multiple steps – e.g. 'forward 7' will be problematic for some pupils who have SLD and/or autism. The nature of their learning difficulty, their ability to process information and their understanding of language all need to be addressed when considering the relevance and purpose of learning activities for these pupils.

For this group of pupils, the benefit of this activity lay in the opportunities it gave them to interact with adults and their peers in a structured and playful way, which helped them to develop their social and language skills. By providing visual supports for the commands, a clear structure to the activity and keeping the language used by adults simple, all the pupils were able to engage with the Robot Games and have fun.

Case study 3: First steps in computational thinking

Many of the aspects of study in Computer Science can be rooted in everyday experiences that offer ways of connecting the key concepts of the subject with what learners already know and understand, much of which is about putting things into an order as to what follows next. Key topics for teaching will include the following.

- **Lists** – Making a list – for instance, establishing the different elements of a task. For example, when cooking, the ingredients in a recipe all go to make up the final dish and often need to be added in a specific order.

- **Sequences** – We have established sequences of action in our lives and in our classrooms. When lessons are winding up ready for breaktime, we often have learners tidying up, then sitting in readiness, perhaps having a snack, then putting on coats and lining up in a given order before leaving the room. At home, we can talk about activities such as getting ready for school, making a sandwich and brushing our teeth.

- **Instructions** – These are similar to sequences, but are given to others, or received from them and acted on – the fundamental activity of coding. These could be about crossing the road safely, navigating to the school office, or turning on the television and finding a programme to watch. They require clarity and progression in order to achieve a successful outcome.

- **Patterns** – Patterns help us to understand repetition and regularity, and how one thing necessarily follows another. Just as in coding an on-screen turtle to draw a regular geometric shape by repeating a series of instructions, so learners can start by arranging counters according to a repeated colour pattern, or even lining up for break in a boy/girl/boy/girl line. The pattern puts order into the task.

- **Logic** – Essential for problem-solving in computing, this is how we make sense of tasks. First, we work out how a result comes about, then create our own step-by-step instructions, with all the variations that might ensue. In crossing the road, for instance, we might think about the hazards and why we need guidance at all. From there, we can discuss different types of crossing, such as zebra crossings and pelican crossings, and how guidance changes when these are available. We might also look at traffic junctions and how traffic lights regulate traffic, or the expectations of drivers at a roundabout. We can explain that the rules of the Highway Code have come about as logical answers to potential dangers.

- **Algorithms** – Despite the seemingly very technical vocabulary, algorithms are part of the Key Stage 1 National Curriculum expectations. It is simply a term that means a set of instructions designed to bring about the same result every time. *An algorithm is a precisely defined procedure – a **sequence** of instructions, or a set of rules, for performing a specific task (e.g. instructions for changing a wheel or making a sandwich). While all correct algorithms should produce the right answer, some algorithms are more efficient than others* (Computing at School, 2013).

While there might be a degree of hierarchy in the development of these skills – for instance, we could begin with making lists, progress to sequences, then on to instructions and finish with creating an algorithm – we might find that we need to come to them repeatedly from different perspectives in order to aid the learner's appreciation and understanding of them. However, given the range of activities presented here, at some level, just about every child and young person can achieve within the Computing curriculum.

Everyday sequencing at The Bridge School

Learning how to use everyday technologies is a computing module that provides pupils who have severe learning difficulties and/or autism at The Bridge School with opportunities to increase their understanding of the world around them and to develop practical skills that will help them to become more independent. It may also help pupils to develop computational thinking by stressing the importance of correct sequencing and demonstrating how changing the steps in a sequence (debugging) can improve the outcome of a task (algorithm) when things go wrong. The module begins with an exploration of the technologies that are in the school itself such as lifts, CCTV and entry systems, before moving on to technologies that are found in the home and the wider community.

Every week the pupils explore a different technology in a practical way, then complete a differentiated worksheet to show what they have learned. Some pupils use symbolised worksheets that ask them to identify the item they have used, what they have used it for and how it is controlled. Others are asked to sequence the steps that they have to take to undertake a task using the technology.

The practical nature of these lessons works well for pupils who learn best in a kinaesthetic way and most pupils enjoy 'making things work' – the microwave popcorn lesson is particularly popular. The importance of sequencing (carrying out the algorithm) is made explicit through questioning using simple language – e.g. 'what next?' – and allowing the pupils to make mistakes (within the boundaries of safety) and then put them right (debugging).

Taking a series of photos or video clips to capture the steps in an everyday sequence can be a great way to consolidate (and provide evidence of) learning. Some pupils really enjoy taking photos and are excellent photographers. These can be used for a variety

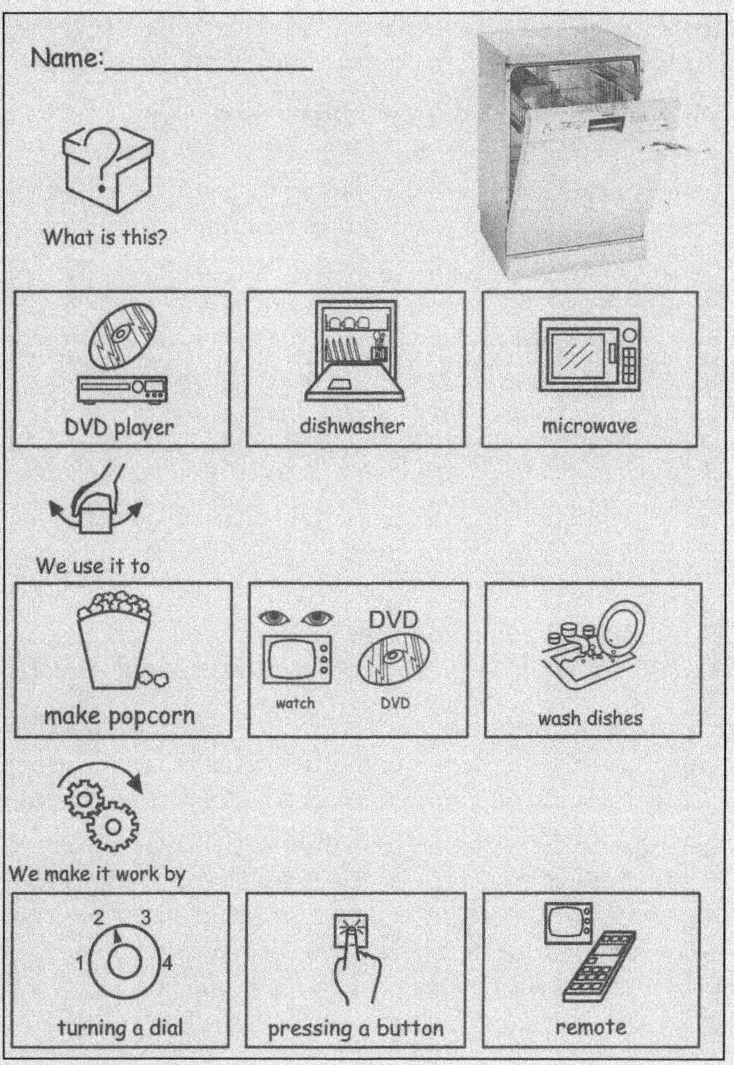

Figure 7.3a Dishwasher worksheet

Figure 7.3b The microwave popcorn lesson

of ordering and sequencing activities ranging from pupils putting laminated photos in the correct order or putting the photos into a PowerPoint presentation, to pupils putting video clips together to make a 'how to' movie.

There are numerous opportunities to carry out practical tasks that involve a step-by-step process throughout the school day and these can be used to encourage pupils to become more aware of the importance of correct sequencing. For example, when washing hands, making a snack or getting dressed after swimming, pupils can be encouraged to identify and carry out the next step with a view to eventually carrying out the entire task independently. Learning to approach tasks as a series of steps is a strategy that can help pupils to become more independent. Visual cues such as symbols showing the steps required can be really helpful. Learning that you could try a different step when things go wrong is a problem-solving skill that a few pupils may be able to generalise into different situations.

Case study 4: Getting started with programming

Computer Science is fundamentally about coding, creating programs through which we control digital devices. One aspect of this is learning the various processes of computational thinking, the ability to approach a problem in structured, systemic ways and to find solutions through technology. Aspects of this include: the logic necessary to predict and analyse; the ability to decompose, to break down a process into parts, and to spot patterns and similarities and to refine the process; then the means to abstract – that is, to remove what is not needed. Once the means to address the problem have been identified, there is the need to create algorithms, the steps necessary to bring about a consistent solution. Finally, there is the need to be able to evaluate, to determine whether this has answered the problem and how well it has done so.

Alongside these concepts are a number of approaches, ways in which we can work, including:

- tinkering – experimenting and playing;
- creating – designing and making;
- debugging – finding and fixing errors;
- persevering – keeping going, resilience;
- collaborating – working together.

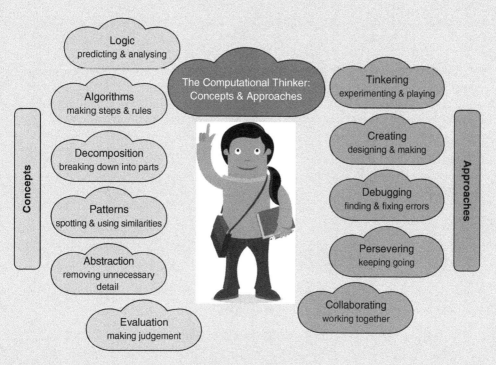

Figure 7.4 Barefoot Computing (www.barefootcas.org.uk)

Coding with dance in Tower Hamlets

Two groups of pupils with moderate learning difficulties attending mainstream schools came together at the Tower Hamlets teachers centre for a term to get started with coding. One activity that proved particularly popular was to create their own version of a dance mat.

We started by watching videos of people playing 'Dance Dance Revolution' to be sure that everyone understood what we were trying to achieve. This was followed up with clips of dancing robots to make the link between programming and dance, with an appreciation that the humans were following an algorithm in the same sense that the robots were.

The children divided into groups of three. Each had a set of cards to place on the floor marked 'Fd, Bk, Lt, Rt,' which were arranged as appropriate in a cross with a blank space in the middle. They were shown how dance moves are often in groups of four, in time with the music, and were asked to create two groups of four movements – two bars of music that were annotated on sugar paper. As part of the exercise, they were introduced to the idea of variables – for instance, 'Lt 2, Fd 2' in one bar and 'Rt 1, Bk 3' in the next.

Once hung on the wall, the sheets of sugar paper became the group's choreography as suitable music was played (Mambo No. 5, in this instance) and we all followed along.

At this point, further variables were introduced, including 'Pause', and two options to 'Finish when done' and 'Finish when the music stops'.

Each of the small groups then created a second iteration of their moves – now of four bars – and were brought back together for another group performance. While this was not a particularly polished performance, everyone experienced the idea of following the sequence, of looping to start again, or finishing a particular sequence then moving on, and of the need to end when the music stopped. They also had a lot of fun.

Reflective questions

- Is there a threshold of understanding necessary before children and young people can engage with the Computing curriculum?

    At one level we can consider whether there are learners for whom Computer Science is an element of the curriculum which is beyond their comprehension. However, the threshold for those who can participate in computing at some level and those who can't may be difficult to discern. The very basis of our control of technology is to click a switch, to activate power, to make something work – the fundamental requirement for us to take command of a machine or device. So developing the ability and understanding to deliberately make something happen using an electrical input could be argued to be the first concept necessary to learn about the subject.

    However, it could be argued that an appreciation of cause and effect is not an aspect of the computing curriculum, and that what is needed is the ability to use technology purposefully, to bring about a particular outcome, to solve a problem.

- Does the study of Computing offer particular benefits to learners with SEND?

    When we think about learners with SEND, there are many ways in which the discipline of Computer Science may have something to offer that other subjects don't: the need for precision in language; the chance to engage in problem solving; the necessity of working in a structured, linear, way; the opportunity to work collaboratively; anticipating an outcome and planning a route to achieve it.

    Computing may offer learning experiences that won't be gained in the rest of the curriculum.

- Do we need screens to teach Computing?

    Turning on a computer screen may not be the best place to start when teaching the concepts of computing. In fact, this could create an additional barrier to learning by requiring understanding of how the hardware and software work before engaging with the subject.

As can be seen from the Robot Games case study, learning about coding and programming can begin some distance from the screen.

Discussion

Computer Science as a special subject for SEND

When coding and programming, there is a need for precision in language and grammar, with specific vocabulary needed to bring about the desired result. If we are not accurate, then nothing happens or the wrong thing does and we get an error message. This discipline may help learners with speech language and communication to gain an understanding of how language works more generally.

We may think that this need for precision will cause particular difficulties for learners with dyslexia. However, coding means working in a language with strict grammar and no exceptions, nothing to trip you up with illogical spelling or structures. Along with difficulties with handling text, this condition is also thought to engender lateral thinking, something that can help get round difficulties when coding. The traits of the condition could become a benefit in Computer Science.

Similarly, people with autistic spectrum conditions are sometimes thought to develop obsessions, close and persisting exploration in often narrow areas of interest, coupled with an insistence on adherence to particular ways of behaving. When coding, this could become an advantage as it provides the resilience necessary to test and retest every aspect of a program to ensure the required outcome. When testing fails, it can provide the perseverance to track down and debug the issue, no matter how deep down in the code it is.

And does programming and controlling a device – a robot arm, for instance – offer learners with disabilities a chance to control aspects of their environment when their own bodies may find it difficult to do so?

There is have been some spectacular advances recently in the ways in which technology can help people to overcome disabilities, from the widespread use of cochlear implants to overcome hearing loss, developments in prosthetic limbs connecting directly to the nervous system, and even cameras and light sensors being connected to the optic nerve to improve visual impairments. Those with physical disabilities and sensory impairments are often early adopters of new technologies, recognising its ability to help them overcome problems in their lives. Computer Science offers a way in which they can become directly involved in its on-going development.

This is a subject with its own particular set of characteristics; in particular, it has a focus on problem solving. In almost every activity there is a need to find a way to get something to happen. While finding the answers there is a need for exploration, to try things out to see what happens. There is often more than one solution to a problem, providing opportunities for creativity, and working with others helps us to share, collaborate and develop ideas. Yet it also has a need for precision in execution in order to get things to happen as we wish. Although along the way there might be plenty of frustration, successfully solving the problem, whether it is having a floor robot navigate a route, changing the look and feel of a web page or creating a computer game, brings the satisfaction of success, and with it a growth of self-confidence and preparedness to meet fresh challenges.

Progression: unplugged activities

Having experienced the situation of role-playing robots, and appreciating the principle of controlling movement by providing directions, more structure can be brought to bear through the use of a simple 2 × 2 grid, initially for the pupils to guide each other around, then later on to use with a programmable toy or floor robot.

Many primary school playgrounds have simple grids already marked out on the tarmac; where there isn't one they are easy to create, indoors or out, using chalk or masking tape. A square of about 2-metre long sides should be about right. With this in place, pupils can pair up and, as with the robot activities, direct each other around it, perhaps from one corner to the diagonal opposite, or around the perimeter. Initially, this will be one step at a time, but lines of instruction can be introduced gradually.

Many pupils will find it difficult to give, or to hear and retain, the list of five steps that would be the minimum to get from one corner to the opposite one. However, these could be modelled by one guiding another one step at a time with each step being recorded, either written on a dry-wipe board, or laid on the ground as a sequence of directional cards (simple arrows will suffice at the early stages) which provide a record of the movement, and hence an initial set of instructions. As they progress, most learners will become more able to work out a route mentally, recording each step as they go, before giving the instructions to a classmate to carry out.

Initially, a simple program to get to the opposite corner might be 'Forward, Forward, Right, Forward, Forward'. As they progress, pupils can add the number of steps and degrees in a turn. 'Forward 2, Right 90, Forward 2'.

Some members of the group might require additional challenge, such as:

- start facing backwards;

- use exactly seven (or another number) commands;

- don't use specific intersections of the grid;

- take the longest possible route without traversing the same line twice.

The intention is to encourage creating a set of instructions, precision in the directions – the language – used, and moving towards the method used for coding on-screen.

Other activities focused on developing an understanding of moving from one point to another by following a list of instructions that could involve the mat from a game of Twister. This has four columns of six dots, each column being a single colour (red, green, blue or yellow). Activities might include groups being given a random selection of coloured cards that they have to put into an order that, when enacted, will move a player from one end to the other on adjacent dots, without moving diagonally. The mat can also be used as a way to simply move from one point to another (as with the 2×2 grid), except there is the option of the grid size used being varied. By folding it to hide some dots, grids from 2×2 to 4×6 can be created.

Another toy that lends itself to unplugged activities is Jenga, the game involving a tower of wooden blocks from which players extract pieces and place them on the top while trying not to let it all fall over. In this activity the focus is not on building a tower, but using language accurately. Working in pairs, each child has two blocks. They sit back to back. One makes a shape with their blocks that they then describe to the other who has to try to re-create it. Working across a group it becomes apparent that a common language helps the process, a common way of describing the orientation of the blocks, and that some shapes – a letter 'T', perhaps – can be given names, rather like a procedure would be in programming that everyone understands and can create uniformly.

Working with familiar toys, even in novel ways, can help connect everyday experiences with Computer Science.

Using toys and floor robots

While unplugged activities are useful to support the development of key concepts in Computer Science and the underpinning notion of computational thinking, those ideas need to be put into practice and the first step is usually through the use of tangible devices.

> *In the form of programmable and interactive robots, computers can become powerful learning tools. Robotics offers children the opportunity to engage with content from the domain of computer science, practice problem-solving skills, and work on fine-motor skills and eye–hand coordination.*

(Umaschi et al., 2014)

One starting point is to use a remote control car. It introduces the idea of having control, but it can also be difficult to get it to do what you want – a helpful comparison to the certainty that comes when you program a floor robot. To emphasise this, it can help to attempt to get both to navigate the same route.

A 2 × 2 grid made with masking tape on a desk makes a connection with earlier activities, with each side being twice the distance a floor robot moves on a single forward button press. To move the car from one corner to its opposite can be more difficult than the robot because it is inconsistent in its movements.

There are a number of floor robots, also referred to as 'turtles' (taken from how the focus on a screen that is controlled in programming languages, such as Logo, is known), on the market. Some, such as the Roamer (www.roamer-educational-robot. com), have been around for many years. Others, such as the popular Bee-Bot (tts-group.co.uk) have not been around as long, but have developed variations from the original model. Others include Sphero (www.sphero.com) and Cubetto (www. primotoys.com).

One criticism might be the potential for confusion between what is a toy and what is a focus for learning. However, what is actually represented is the intrinsic relationship of play and learning, as Mitchel Resnick points out when writing about the development of the Scratch programming language at MIT, designed for children to use.

> *When most people think about play, they think about fun and enjoyment. But when my research group thinks about play, we think about it somewhat differently. We think of play as an attitude and an approach for engaging with the world. We associate play with taking risks, trying new things, and testing boundaries. We see play as a process of tinkering, experimenting, and exploring. These aspects of play are central to the creative learning process.*

(Resnick, 2014)

Cubetto is sold in toy shops across the world, but it is an extremely useful resource for taking early steps in Computer Science in the classroom. It is not programmed directly on the device, but via a tangible interface. This is a wooden panel with a number of slots into which users insert pieces denoting Forward, Left, Right and Function. The program is then transmitted to Cubetto (a small, rudimentary, floor robot made of wood with a large wheel on either side) to follow. The Function refers to a subset of four pieces that can be created on the interface. As Cubetto moves, learners can follow the sequence of moves through the LEDs that light up on each action. It is a device deliberately designed to attract pupils in Early Years settings, but will work for older learners with SEND very well. The tactile nature of its operation and the concrete method of programming make a very clear link between the users' actions and those of the device.

Bee-Bot is similarly a tangible device as pupils program it by pressing buttons on top – Forward, Backward, Left, Right and Pause – then press Go to make it move. The commands and the actions are very closely related, and can be built up one step at a time, although learners will probably need to write down longer strings of commands before keying them in.

A more recent iteration of the Bee-Bot is the Blue-Bot, so called because it includes Bluetooth connectivity, which means that as well as programming using the integral buttons, as before, it can also be programmed remotely using an IOS or Android app. It also has the option of using a Tactile Reader. This is a bar into which up to ten tiles can be slotted, each of which denote an action. Like Cubetto, the coding is done in a very concrete way, and each command can be followed on execution as an LED lights up. Debugging becomes a matter of removing and replacing tiles, which could be physically laid out along a route prior to insertion in the Tactile Reader as part of the process of working out what commands to use. As Umaschi et al. (2014) point out, *by iteratively planning and revising a robotics project in a supportive environment, children may gain confidence in their abilities to learn and solve problems.*

The use of the Blue-Bot app to program the device provides a very useful bridge on to coding on screen. It comes with various backgrounds, all of which can be purchased as floor mats, and activities on the ground can as easily be activities on-screen.

In all these instances the basic 2×2 grid provides a flexible starting point for a number of activities. Bigger grids and commercially produced mats can develop this activity, although there is plenty of flexibility in how they can be used with various tasks and activities on offer, such as obstacle courses, making it dance to music and helping it to find its way between places.

Working on the screen

Ultimately, coding is an activity that happens on a computer screen, and teaching pupils to code in languages such as Scratch or Logo while sitting at a machine is the eventual goal. However, along the way there are numerous resources that can help achieve this.

Pupils at The Bridge School who have severe learning difficulties and/or autism, for instance, learn about sequencing and problem solving, which lie at the root of Computer Science, by using computer games and apps. One resource, Help Kidz Learn (www.helpkidzlearn.com), is a comprehensive set of online learning activities designed for pupils who have SEND and are working below National Curriculum expectations. It includes a number of games that help pupils to begin to develop problem-solving skills. A favourite with pupils who are learning to access the computer is the Cupcakeinator game which allows the user to create cakes, first by moving a cake case along a conveyor belt, through selecting target 1, to get it to the correct place where, by selecting target 2 (the algorithm) they can fill it with cake mix. Selecting the wrong target results in a mess, so the user can see if they made a correct choice and the person supporting the pupil can see whether or not they are able to correct (debug) their mistakes in subsequent attempts.

Another favourite is Busythings (www.busythings.co.uk), a website packed with online activities created for pupils in mainstream early years and primary education that can be used by learners with a very broad range of learning needs and none. Some of the games involve position and direction, and sequencing; these can be used in computing lessons to engage the pupils in problem-solving activities.

Tunnel Trouble is a game that involves moving a chicken through a series of rotating tunnels to get to a gate on the other side. Players have to select and rotate the tunnels to create a pathway. The game can be played at several levels of difficulty. At The Bridge School, by selecting the level of difficulty suitable for each pupil it was possible to play Tunnel Trouble as a whole group activity at a whiteboard as a starter, then offer the game to the pupils on tablets so they could play by themselves. Over six weekly sessions, all pupils made progress with the game, maintained their enthusiasm for it and some even chose to continue playing it when they were given 'choosing time' on the tablets at the end of the lesson.

There are many other games that help to develop computational thinking skills. Line Up requires players to add monsters to a sequence, selecting shape and colour to correctly complete it, while Block-a-doodle-do is a logic activity requiring users to aid the progress of a car by removing other vehicles parked in its path. There is also Path Peril, which is a first step in coding. A chicken has to navigate a maze and collect lozenges of differing shapes and colours along the way. By creating a path using command arrows, similar to those on the Bee-Bot, pupils have to guide it safely through the maze, avoiding hazards and greedy monsters, and safely out of the door. All these activities can be set at different levels and will automatically progress to greater degrees of difficulty.

There are several resources that offer routes in to more formal coding. Crystal Rainforest is one of a selection of online games within the Crystal ICT Channel (www.sherston.com/crystal), which provides an introduction to Logo programming in the context of an adventure game set in a rainforest. Pupils at The Bridge School have been using this game in weekly computing lessons to learn about coding in an accessible and enjoyable way. The narrative (players have to find crystals to save the king who has been poisoned by loggers who are destroying the rainforest against his command) is engaging and makes a great whiteboard starter for each lesson. The activities, which can be undertaken at two levels of difficulty, give pupils lots of practice at using simple logo commands when working at their own workstations.

Another widely used resource offering a structured approach to learning coding is 2Code, part of 2Simple's Purplemash (www.purplemash.com). This provides sets of on-screen tasks that pupils follow, each of which ends with an open activity for them to experiment with the code they now know. It is designed for use by classes where the teacher is very limited in their knowledge of the subject, so it is very detailed and highly structured, and covers the whole primary age-range.

A less prescriptive, but also progressive, offer comes from J2E with their J2Code. This provides on-screen activities that closely relate to the method of programming floor robots, and progresses through accessible versions of both Logo and Scratch, to fully using these programming languages by the end of primary school.

Tynker Coding for Kids (www.tynker.com) is designed to teach children to code through graded activities that are fun and motivating. A group of pupils at The Bridge School have been using Candy Quest, a beginner's game, to learn about coding using block code. These were pupils who have demonstrated an interest in, and aptitude for, problem-solving games involving sequencing, position and direction on the computer. Players have to use block code commands to complete a task set for their character, the tasks becoming increasingly complex. The pupils were all able to progress through the game, although not all understood the 'repeat' function and preferred to add multiple blocks rather than use repeat.

Also online is a wealth of resources at www.code.org. This has many activities for a very diverse range of learners. A number of courses teach different aspects of coding and offer introductions to various languages through activities based around familiar scenarios, including the Angry Birds app, the computer game Minecraft and the Disney movie *Frozen*. There are also suggestions for unplugged activities and videos to engage learners and support teachers.

Beyond this, there are also several apps worth investigating, all of which run on iPads, not forgetting the Bee-Bot and Blue-Bot offerings. Lightbot is a puzzle involving the need to program a path for a robot to move around a 3D maze that becomes progressively more challenging. Daisy the Dinosaur provides a simple introduction to using blocks of code, while Scratch Junior is a useful way to begin to program in that particular language.

Summary and Key Points

Computing is a subject that offers a unique range of learning opportunities to pupils with a very diverse range of learning needs. While programming might be conceived of as a narrow, tightly disciplined activity, it can be approached in a broad and creative way, both on- and off-screen.

> *Because the tangible programs and robots exist off-screen, children are drawn to investigate the work of other children, work collaboratively, and negotiate sharing materials, as well as develop their fine-motor skills. These artifacts serve as points of discussion and reminders of the activity content even after the computer has been turned off . . . in this rich process of creation in both the physical and digital worlds, children actively engage in problem-solving and learn powerful ideas from computer science and robotics, including core concepts of computational thinking.*
>
> (Umaschi et al., 2014)

Learners benefit from a better appreciation of technology in the world around them, activities that develop problem-solving skills, new approaches to using language, chances to co-operate and collaborate with others, and lots of fun.

While this is a discipline that may be thought of as precise, constrained and restricted in its content, as can be seen, it lends itself to imaginative, creative approaches that connect with pupils' understanding and experience of the world around them.

Useful links

The Bridge is a teaching school with a reputation for its training and research: www.thebridgelondon. co.uk

Computing at School and Barefoot Computing have produced a site to support primary computing: https://barefootcas.org.uk

A group of professionals interested in ensuring that Computing as a subject is taught inclusively contribute to the #CASinclude group: www.computingatschool.org.uk/custom_pages/270-cas-include

The code.org website provides a host of on-screen resources to teach coding, along with explanatory videos and ideas for 'unplugged' approaches.

References

Bers, MU, Flannery, L, Kazakoff, ER and Sullivan, A (2014) Computational thinking and tinkering: Exploration of an early childhood robotics curriculum. *Computers & Education*, 72.

Computing at School (2013) *Computing in the National Curriculum: A Guide for Primary Teachers*.

Galpin, J (2015) *Easy as Pi*, special children magazine edition, 223, March/April.

Imray, P and Colley, A (2017) *Inclusion is Dead: Long Live Inclusion*. Basingstoke: Routledge.

Resnick, M (2014) Give P's a chance: Projects, peers, passion, play. Paper presented at Constructionism and Creativity, Vienna.

Chapter 8

ART

REBECCA HEATON AND JEAN EDWARDS

Introduction

Creative arts pedagogies and practices in education enable criticality (Nilson et al., 2013). They enhance cognitive development (Eisner, 2002; Efland, 2002), assist in building communities (Lawton, 2014) and facilitate engagement with lived and virtual worlds (Wegerif, 2012). With these factors in mind, the contribution the creative arts makes to education becomes clearer. However, despite this, in England the creative arts in education continue to be marginalised (Adams and Hiett, 2012; Pooley and Rowell, 2016; NSEAD, 2016). In this chapter we exemplify how and why technology should be embedded in the creative arts, with a specific focus on the subject area of art and design. We conceptualise what the creative arts and art are, demonstrate how physical and digital approaches to art making, teaching and learning can be used and interwoven to facilitate practice for mainstream and special education settings, and model the interdisciplinary nature of the arts. Through doing this, we reiterate the need for the creative arts in education and disseminate the message that creativity is central to creative arts practice due to its value as a life skill, form of intelligence and tool for economic growth (McLellan and Nicholl, 2013). We identify the importance of an attitude focused on possibility thinking (Craft, 2013) to enable all learners, regardless of personal, social, emotional, mental or physical need, to succeed in learning in, through and about the creative arts, and discuss how technology is central to this. Technology and its associated tools and practices are embedded throughout the content of this chapter. In the arts in education, technology is not seen as a separate entity, individual or additional area of study. It does have the potential to stand alone and be an artistic and educational discipline in its own right, but we make the decision to weave technological practice throughout the creative arts in this chapter to mirror and exemplify how it is positioned, interpreted and can be utilised most effectively in the English primary National Curriculum to date (DfE, 2013).

In the English primary curriculum (DfE, 2013) for Art and Design and other creative arts subjects (Music and PE–Dance) there is no, or in the case of music, little reference to a requirement to study technology. While this appears problematic, because if taken at face value technological practice in the arts would not occur, or perhaps only at the discretion of the passionate or forward-thinking teacher, the issue can also be seen to pass ownership to the practitioner to align their subject with the contemporary world. This is beneficial because the curriculum is broad enough for a skilled teacher to read between the lines and both identify and respond to technological developments in their curriculum content. For example, in art and design the curriculum requires pupils to know how art facilitates and responds to culture. In today's world, this would require emphasis on the study of technology. For a creative arts curriculum to be successful it requires purpose, expression and innovation; it requires teachers and pupils to be open to technological development and the needs underpinned by the use of established and emerging digital tools that are developed and used to respond to cultural change (Hickman and Heaton, 2016; Heaton, n.d.). If this can be achieved across the arts in mainstream and special education settings, pupil learning will be enhanced because learning in the creative arts disciplines and special education (Liu et al., 2013) that uses, is fuelled by and develops technology, makes learning relevant to life and positions learners as creators and creative developers in their globalised world (Patton and Buffington, 2016; Heaton, n.d.).

Throughout this chapter, we refer to a number of teaching and learning strategies that can be used as central components to develop an effective digital offering in the primary creative arts classroom to aid in achieving the aims above. These include provision of interconnected physical and digital creative arts experiences, consideration of the roles of process and product in the facilitation and progression of learning, and the effectiveness of interdisciplinarity in enhancing technological connectivity and, ultimately, skill enhancement for pupil and teacher. We reiterate these themes in our chapter learning objectives, exemplify them in a class context in three cases, and explain their contribution to learning in detail in our discussion. When reading this chapter we hope to provide you with fundamental principles and teaching ideas that can be adapted and interwoven into creative arts offerings as singular or cross-curricular and cultural experiences.

Learning objectives

By the end of this chapter you should be able to:

- understand the relationship between physical to digital processes and tools;
- develop an awareness of process and product with a focus on assessment and accessibility for both maker and audience;
- consider collaboration and connectivity working in interdisciplinary ways and learning from others.

Links to Teachers' Standards

2. Promote good progress and outcomes by pupils
3. Demonstrate good curriculum and subject knowledge
4. Plan and teach well structured lessons
5. Adapt teaching to respond to the strengths and needs of all pupils
6. Make accurate and productive use of assessment

(DfE, 2011, p. 1)

Links to National Curriculum Programmes of Study (Art)

- produce creative work, exploring ideas and recording experiences;
- become proficient in drawing, painting, sculpture and other art, craft and design techniques;
- evaluate and analyse creative works using the language of art, craft and design;
- know about great artists, craft makers and designers, and understand the historical and cultural development of their art forms.

(DfE, 2013, p. 1)

Links to National SENCo Standards

4. Strategies for improving outcomes for pupils with SEN and/or disabilities:

    - removing barriers to participation and learning for children and young people with SEN and/or disabilities;
    - the potential of new technologies to support communication, teaching and learning for children and young people with SEN and/or disabilities.

9. Develop, implement, monitor and evaluate systems to:

    - record and review the progress of children and young people with SEN and/or disabilities.

Part C: There are high expectations for all children and young people with SEN and/or disabilities.

(NCTL, 2014, pp. 6, 7, 8)

Case study 1: Swap and share

In this case study, children use a combination of physical and digital art techniques to create, manipulate, transform and develop imagery. They share their artwork in person and online, creating a community of art practice resulting from the swapping and sharing of images.

Pupil learning outcomes

By participating in an image swap the children will:

- manipulate physical and digital imagery;
- respond to art made by others;
- reflect on the process and outcome.

Technology required

Children will need access to the camera on a tablet or other mobile device. They will use a range of tools and apps to manipulate images: these could be a Tiny Planet app such as Rollworld (IOS) or Tiny Planet, a photo manipulation app such as Fragment (IOS and Android) and the web tool Pictaculous (www.pictaculous.com). They will draw or paint on to their image using a drawing or painting app. They will need a photo collage app or tool such as Pic Collage (IOS and Android) so that they can add each new image to their photo collage. A QR code maker and reader and Google photos will also be useful at the sharing stage.

Pupil activity

In this case study, children worked over half term on a series of images, collaborating around the class as they moved through the stages outlined in the app flow shown in the table below.

In this series of art explorations children are able to transform images made by themselves and their friends without losing the original images. Technology frees them to take risks and make dramatic changes knowing that their original work is protected. They can compare and identify changes, linking these to the tools and processes they have used. Swapping art with others in this safe environment allows children to encounter a range of different starting points and helps them to experience and understand artistic collaboration. Quite quickly children move away from recognisable and representative images and start to work with shape, pattern and colour, leading to more abstract images that use the functions of the apps and tools the teacher has selected. This immediately helps overcome the concern some children have of creating art that 'looks like' something and judging themselves on account of this. At the end of the activity each child has a photo collage of the images they have made so that they can reflect upon their swaps, scaffolded by some prompts. Each child can also track the journey of their images as they appear in the art made by others, leading to discussion of how artists work together and how ideas flow between artists. The collages can be shared by uploading them to Googlephotos and attaching each to a QR code. This will allow children and parents to view the images at school and at home, as well as being a way of adding the digital artwork to the child's sketchbook or art folder.

Variations and related activities

This activity can be developed and changed by substituting different tools into the steps. It may be that the steps and tools are all focused on one theme, such as nature or buildings, or one element of art such as colour or pattern. Connections to science can be made perhaps through exploring magnification as a connecting theme (Edwards, 2014b). For older pupils or those needing a greater challenge, choice can be built in at each step. For pupils with specific needs, these can be considered at each step and

Table 8.1 Steps in swapping and sharing imagery

	What did the children do?	Technology
Step 1	Take a photo of something meaningful to you. Save it as the first picture in a photo collage. Pass the photo on to someone in your class.	Camera Photo collage app
Step 2	Take your new photo and manipulate it using the app Rollworld. Pass it back to the child you got it from. Add the photo you get back to your photo collage and also pass it on to someone else.	Camera roll Photo collage app Rollworld
Step 3	Take your new photo and put it into the website Pictaculous using 'get my palette'. Take your palette of colours and use them to make a piece of art (collage, drawing or painting). Pass it back to the child you got it from. Add the photo you get back to your photo collage and also pass it on to someone else.	Camera roll Photo collage app (www.pictaculous.com) (art materials)
Step 4	Take your new photo and make a change to it using the app Fragment. Pass it back to the child you got it from. Add the photo you get back to your photo collage and also pass it on to someone else.	Camera roll Photo collage app Fragment app
Step 5	Take your new photo and make a change to it using a drawing or painting app. Pass it back to the child you got it from. Add the photo you get back to your photo collage and also pass it on to someone else.	Drawing or painting app Photo collage app Fragment app
Step 6	Have a look at your photo collage, which should now have five images that you worked on (one from each step). Look for and talk to the other children you worked with in the swap. Suggested prompts for reflective talk: • My favourite image is . . . because . . . • My favourite week was . . . because . . . • If I was doing this again I would . . . because . . . • I have learned . . . • My advice to others would be . . . Look for the image you started with and see if you can track it through the journey of what other children did with it.	Photo collage app QR code maker and reader Googlephotos

a choice made at the planning stage to use apps and tools that include rather than exclude. The collaborative nature of this activity can be developed much further by swapping across classes in the same school, between schools locally or further afield, and between mainstream and special schools. The digital nature of the activity allows for swapping across large distances and this could be a tool for developing collaboration through eTwinning or other international partnerships.

Figure 8.1 Example of app flow: this can be adjusted to represent your sequence of tools and apps used in image swaps and can be used to help children follow the sequence

Figure 8.2 Example of what could be made

Case study 2: Virtual sculptures

In this case study, children were asked to use common art materials and resources to construct mini sculptures. They then used greenscreen technology to place their sculptures in locations local to them and further away to experiment with scale and space.

Pupil learning outcomes

By making and sharing virtual sculptures, the children will:

- manipulate physical materials on a small scale;

- use a green screen app to manipulate the scale and orientation of their sculptures;

- use a green screen app to place their sculptures in a variety of environments;

- act in the role of an artist by recording supporting artist's information about their sculpture for the viewer.

Technology required

Children will need access to the camera on a tablet or other mobile device. A green screen app will be needed, such as the IOS app Green Screen by Do Ink , or Green Screen Lite or Green Screen Magic on Android. To make an audio commentary, use a voice recorder tool such as audioBoom or the video function on the mobile device being used, or a note-taking app such as Skitch. To share the sculptures in their locations a QR code maker will be necessary and any viewers would need QR code readers on their devices.

Other resources

Some bright green paper, card or fabric are needed to make a do-it-yourself green screen. Art materials or construction toys are needed to make the sculptures.

Pupil activity

In this case study, children started by using familiar materials to make small sculptures. It is useful to restrict the size of the sculptures made by using a rule such as 'no bigger than your hand' or providing a box into which the sculpture must fit. Restricting the size is one way of making sculpture more manageable – many sculptors would make small models (maquettes) of their sculptures to work through their ideas before moving on to make the finished large version. It also prevents children from being overwhelmed by the size of the task. Materials such as card, clay, dough, plasticine, wood and found junk or existing resources such as construction kits or found natural materials can be used. Decisions about what to make the sculptures out of should be guided by the teachers' knowledge of the pupils in relation to their physical abilities to manipulate tools and materials, their prior experience and curriculum requirements such as exploring the work of a particular sculptor.

Having made the sculptures, each sculpture was photographed on a totally green backdrop. Children were taught about viewpoints and supported to take a view that showed their sculpture sitting flat on the surface. It may be necessary to help children keep the device steady and in the right position by marking the position of the device out or using a tripod to steady the camera. After this and using the same device, children photographed locations where their sculptures might sit on their school site or locally.

A Green Screen app was used to place the photos of the sculptures into the photos of the various locations. This is a step-by-step procedure that can be scaffolded by a series of pictures, a short video guide or by training several pupils as digital mentors to support the rest of the class. Each child should then choose one of their completed photos to record a commentary where they provide the information usually available on the gallery label. This should be differentiated to the spoken language level of the children and scaffolded with a speaking frame that outlines what to include and perhaps includes some sentence starters or model sentences. An opportunity to annotate using writing can be offered as an alternative to speaking using a note-taking app such as Skitch.

To share the sculptures with an audience, each photo and recording can be tagged to a QR code. These codes can be placed in the locations where the sculptures are placed in the photos so that children, parents and visitors can use their own mobile devices to view the sculptures virtually and listen to the descriptions provided by the sculptors.

In this case study, children are given the opportunity to communicate by making art out of physical materials, talking about it and by using technology to share both the art and their comments with a wider audience of viewers. This adds meaning and supports engagement with the various stages of the activity. It can be undertaken by individuals, or children might be paired to work together for parts or all of the activity. Collaboration can be further supported by peer review at each stage to allow for advice and mutual support. There are a number of opportunities for children to work independently or be scaffolded towards this with, for example, prompt cards, peer mentors, speaking frames and modelling.

Variations and related activities

This activity can be introduced by sending a letter from someone (the headteacher, a school governor) who would like to commission sculptures for the school site. In this format children can be asked to consider more fully the relationship between the space where their sculpture will sit and what they will make. In this version there is more challenge in terms of exploring and evaluating the relationship between sculpture (form) and the space, as well as how the viewers will feel about it. The large outdoor sculptures by Michael Craig-Martin or Jake and Dinos Chapman could provide a good starting point.

Figure 8.3 Virtual sculpture placed in school grounds and on the fourth plinth in Trafalgar Square, London (created by Standens Barn Primary School, Northampton)

It can also be presented as an opportunity to create sculptures for places further afield. In this version the idea of the fourth plinth in Trafalgar Square could be used (Edwards, 2017), or children could be allowed to choose where in the world they would like to place their sculptures. A Google Map can be used to share the outcomes, tagging each sculpture and description to the map so that the viewer can explore them. In this case, children would need to download photos of places, taking care to use a safe image search such as www.photosforclass.com.

Case study 3: Digital assemblage in conceptual art

In this case study, children learn how to bring meaning to their artwork beyond the aesthetic. They use a range of digital art tools to make personal, social, political and cultural comments and, in doing so, learn how art can portray voice, be persuasive and generate impact.

Pupil learning outcomes

By creating conceptual art and a digital assemblage, the children will:

- learn about the techniques and practices of contemporary artists;

- use their artistic voice to express emotion;

- create a digital artefact in collaboration to comment on an issue;

- use a collaborative digital platform to understand a range of perspectives.

Technology required

Children will need access to the camera on a tablet or other mobile device to take images and record video. Recording apps such as Vine, Viddy and 1TapVideo for IOS and Android can also be used. Internet access will be needed to collaborate on virtual bulletin boards such as Padlet or interact with multimedia launchers like ThingLink. Teachers can facilitate easy access to these tools by using QR code generators and QR readers. A selection of apps to express voice and create digital artefacts is also required; examples include ChatterPix, Morfo, Visual Poetry, Visual Poet, Path on and iMovie.

Other resources

Access to the work of activists (Ai Wei Wei, Anish Kapoor, Banksy and Tanja Bruguera) and social justice or socially engaged artists (Doris Salcedo, Assemble, Favianna Rodriguez, and Bob and Roberta Smith) would be useful.

Pupil activity

The anticipated challenge of this case was finding a way for the children to engage with the concepts behind artwork (to include the work of artists and the children's own) rather than focusing solely on the process or the product of making art. With this in mind, the case study began with the class teacher selecting an issue to be studied through digital art that relates to the pupils' everyday experience. In this case, the Key Stage 2 children considered their transition to a new school, an issue that is accessible, personal and current for the pupils. Lesson one began with the children being asked how they felt about moving to a new school; other issues could be explored here that involve changes in the children's communities, opinions on news stories or environmental concerns, for example. The question was posted to the children via a Padlet (www.padlet.com) accessed via a QR reader. The teacher then asked the children to capture a photograph and post it to the collaborative board that expressed how they felt about their transition (or issue). Very quickly a number of images were being displayed producing a collaborative digital artefact that expressed 30 perspectives on an issue. This encouraged the children to talk about different opinions and points of view, considering the messages behind a piece of artwork rather than the work itself, and provided important learning development when considering conceptual messages in art. The children were then asked where this digital display could be located to maximise its voice and access to it. The children wanted it displayed in the school hall so that other children and parents could engage with it and understand their emotions about the issue being studied. By creating the work using a collaborative online tool, art could easily be shared on a school website or blog once e-safety considerations had been made. Padlet has the facility to post video, online links, images, text and sound clips, so the variations for conceptual content sharing are vast.

The second phase of this case involved the children engaging with the artwork of artist Ai WeiWei. Three works were shared with the children demonstrating his visual voice on the Sichuan earthquake. These included: *Straight*, 2008–2012; #aiflowers; the names of the student earthquake victims found by the victims.

Please note when discussing and selecting artworks, particularly conceptual ones, with children, you need to be mindful of their needs and circumstances, as some issues can be challenging to address. Works appropriate to your children's needs should be used.

The children were challenged to consider what Ai Weiwei was expressing and how he had used his voice as an artist to share his thoughts. This experience provided the foundation for the creation of the children's own digital artefacts and assemblages explained next.

As a class, the children were studying environmentalism, and through their digital artwork the children considered what it meant to be an environmentally conscious citizen. Although environmentalism was explored in this case, any social, cultural or political issue could be engaged with to offer this experience. Individually, the children were asked to create a digital artefact using either a digital recording tool or app, or Visual Poet, Path on, Chatter Pix, Morfo or Visual Poetry to comment on or provide an example that illuminated the issue being explored. At this stage you could limit or extend the number or type of software options offered to the children to express their voice, select ones appropriate to their SEND and to their skill in using the software. You may need to teach how to use the digital tool first. When the children had created their responses individually, they were grouped and challenged to review and combine their ideas into a ThingLink, iMovie or Padlet. By creatively working in collaboration, the children were challenged to explain their thinking and concept to one another; they had to use empathy, observe from a different perspective and be open to their artwork changing and evolving. These are some of the skills and considerations that conceptual artists use when designing, making and performing their creations. The children in the case were positioning themselves as young conceptual artists and were enthused by making artwork that was purposeful, responsive to contemporary life and that utilised the tools of the modern digital world.

Variations and related activities

This activity also works successfully when physical art mediums are combined with the digital, as children can create physical artworks to be used in their digital creations. There is scope to consider the relevance of exhibition spaces in conceptual works of art. The children can share their digital creations with different audiences and in multiple locations. The activity can be extended by collaborating with another school virtually or in person, so that children can be exposed to the problems, issues, concerns and opinions of others on local, national and international platforms, broadening their cultural understanding and awareness of contemporary society. In an assembly, a whole school's perspective on an issue can quickly be captured and, if digitally shared, this can extend to the wider school community. If in simplifying this activity, one child's attitude or emotions to an issue over time can be captured, documented and referred back to showing development or regression in opinions or ideas, it can assist them in understanding the concepts of time or change.

Reflective questions

- How do physical art-making processes and digital technology work together in your planning and teaching (focus on including all pupils)?

- How can digital technology support your approach to assessment?

- How can digital technology support you in connecting with others (pupils, teachers, schools) near and far?

Discussion

A focus on progression, teaching, learning and assessment

As discussed in the introduction and model in the case studies, children learn art in many ways, such as through making, reflecting, collaborating, experiencing, revisiting and researching (Edwards 2014a; Hickman and Heaton, 2015). This learning can be intrinsic and extrinsic, and can occur in or through the arts (Fleming, 2012). Art also has the facility to develop learners' social, emotional, moral and cultural understanding (Gast, 2015). Identifying learning in art and the arts is complex. It is further complicated by a saturation of sensory content in our interdisciplinary environments and developmental digital world. For mainstream learners and those with SEND learning in such environments, apart from understanding the learning occurring, is a challenge. Table 8.1 conceptualises how learning in art can occur in the cases we share in this chapter. We draw on the Studio Habits of Mind framework (Hetland et al., 2007) found at: http://ccsesaarts.org/wp-content/uploads/2015/01/Studio-Habits-of-Mind.pdf to exemplify how learning occurs in each case. What you can observe from our table is that through each case we have discussed, skill progression occurs in relation to each habit of mind as the cases build up. Learners are able to access the habits of mind in each case activity in a different way, fundamental art skills, such as the studio learning habits and concepts such as texture and scale, are revisited but also reworked and reapplied in different contexts consolidating and embedding skills for learners.

Table 8.2 An identification of studio habit progression in three digital art cases

Studio habits of mind (Hetland *et al.*, 2007)	Case 1: Swap and share	Case 2: Virtual sculptures	Case 3: Digital assemblage
Stretch and explore	Playing with new digital manipulation techniques	Experimenting virtually with scale and location	Trialling new ideas and concepts through digital making
Express	Making an action or abstract response in relation to your own or another's work	Responding to a time or place	Creating a digital artefact to express a feeling towards an idea
Develop craft	Using apps to create and abstract imagery	Using Green Screen technology to explore space	Using the artistic convention of analysis to reveal concepts digitally
Envision	Picturing or understanding a physical or digital action before it occurs; transitioning between the real and the abstract	Trialling and reviewing sculptures in different locations to reach a decision	Depicting a concept in a mental, visual, digital or sensory form
Understand the arts community	Interacting with others in the class and online	Creating dialogue with those in another locality or environment	Interacting with others (artists, peers and society) to understand and solve problems
Observe	Using fundamental art skills (e.g. shape, scale and texture) to look in different ways	Visualising environments and spaces differently (such as scale and texture)	Presenting new or alternative perspectives on issues
Engage and persist	Persevering by swapping, changing and editing art	Focusing to understand a location or environment in which to position a sculpture	Identifying social problems and using art to unpick, respond and change them
Reflect	Using digital making as a reflective device and voice	QR codes reveal a response or reflection on process or product	Collaborate and make judgements about your own and others' perceptions

The National Society for Education in Art and Design have also produced *A Framework for Progression, Planning for Learning, Assessment, Recording and Reporting* (NSEAD, 2014a) that can support teachers in identifying and implementing quality experiences for their learners in art and design. Whichever research-informed guidance a school, teacher or learner chooses to adopt to support the implementation of progression in their art learning experiences, it must be appropriate to the needs of the learner being taught, so it may be appropriate to draw from a range of frameworks in collaboration. The P Scale Art and Design Performance descriptors (DfE, 2017, pp. 5–6) provide a foundation in art for SEND pupils from 5 to 16 working below National Curriculum (DfE, 2013) standards, and actually present a number of skills and concepts that can be accessed through digital art making and its associated practices. The Training Development Agency (TDA, 2010) also produced subject guidance to support practitioners to offer inclusive practices and experiences to pupils with SEN or Learning Disabilities in Primary Art and Design. This document is now dated, specifically in relation to digital learning content and assistive technologies, but does bring to the fore strategies that teachers should be aware of when planning, teaching and assessing for SEND learners in this subject.

To provide more up-to-date examples of how technology can be used to support learners with more complex special educational needs or disabilities, we revisit the cases we have discussed and explain how, gesture-based learning, through the use of Leap Motion or Kinect, can be used to enable such learners to access the experiences we put forward. Gesture-based tools can enable learners to express voice through drawing in the air, or enable them to affect or make comment on, or in response to, their own environments or stimuli through their ability to mirror movements made. Software, like Visikord or ReacTickles, used in conjunction with gesture-based technologies can enable pupils to turn sound or movement into expressive and visually captivating outputs. If used as part of or in relation to the cases we discuss, learners with complex learning difficulties would be able to make art digitally that, in the sketchbook circles example, responds to one of their own or another's photographs. They could make their expressions by layering their gestures on top of imagery previously created. This would allow the learner to use a communicative voice that made a response to their own or others' learning and the contemporary educational world. In the case of the virtual sculptures, their drawings could become the sculptures themselves, or their voices, expressed through sound or visuals, could be used to comment on the sculptures in situ. This would increase pupil awareness of environments and enable them to see purposeful uses for their creative outputs. In the third case concerning an understanding of conceptual art, the software could be used to make emotional responses to the works of other artists or their peers' practice, or to conceptualise their own ideas into sounds or abstract images. Teachers will need to tailor the use of these tools to the needs of their specific learners and extend or simplify their suggestions to ensure that they are accessible and purposeful for learning.

When engaging in art, assessment on behalf of the learner and teacher needs to occur to enable development. However, assessment in art is a controversial practice (Ní Bhroin, 2015; Robins, 2016) and teachers often lack confidence and understanding to engage in this process at a deep level. This is not surprising when art developments in the modern world create controversy and debate, and National Curriculum (DfE, 2013) levels and benchmarks have been removed. However, as with learning in art, assessment too can occur in different manners. A number of approaches, such as assessment through critique, through artefact and the symbiosis of making and criticality are discussed in the visual art chapter by Hickman and Heaton (2015). Teachers often debate whether it is process or product that should be assessed, process referring to the stages of making and development, but also to research, questions, reflections and alterations made during an artistic journey. Teachers of young children particularly and learners often ask 'what is the art of?' as opposed to 'what is the art for?' The second question provides more scope for a learner to critique, reconsider and ultimately produce a piece of art that is personal and responsive to their current or future time and existence. The tool kit developed by Gast (2012) that explores effective questioning and talk in primary art – see: www.nsead.org/downloads/Effective_Questioning&Talk.pdf – is an excellent resource to support teachers in developing dialogue, intervention opportunities and scaffolded environments to support teaching, learning and assessment during and in response to art experiences. When the process of making is documented using digital technology or is made digitally, including oral or written commentary by the child, there is richer material for assessment available than with just an end product which, for many children, may not demonstrate the learning and progress they have made.

In the case studies above, there are a number of opportunities to build in assessment using the features of technology to support this. In Case Study 1, the sequence of images created by the child provide evidence of the child's use of technology, art techniques and self-evaluation when the child chooses which image to keep and take forward. In Case Study 2, as well as the artefact created, there is opportunity for children to communicate their intentions and reflect upon their purpose using a note-taking app (Skitch) or by recording spoken language using a frame of reflective and self-evaluative questions. In Case Study 3, there is the opportunity for teacher and child to use the same tool (Padlet) to provide feedback, as well as the opportunity to engage in peer dialogue. In these case studies and, indeed, in other sequences of art activity whether digital or not, the tools of digital technology can support assessment such as when a teacher uses a time-lapse approach to help children recall their process and see it emerge and develop over time.

Summary and Key Points

This chapter has discussed embedding digital technologies in art and design with a focus on inclusion. The Manifesto for Art, Craft and Design Education (NSEAD, 2014b, p. 6) includes art in its seven policy proposals, noting *the inclusive, diverse, transformational and restorative power of the visual arts*. With the addition of digital technologies, the potential for inclusion only increases. The possibilities available to us in the classroom to use devices, apps and tools in learning and teaching in art are developing constantly, providing us as teachers and our learners with opportunities to explore creatively and use processes that only a few years ago would have been unavailable to us in the classroom, extending the already inclusive nature of the subject even further. It is vital that we as teachers endeavour to keep our subject knowledge up to date as the technology develops. As the NSEAD (2012, p. 1) outline of the 21st-century teacher suggested, we must *use technology to offer greater flexibility and choice, delivering lessons that use a wide range of teaching techniques and differentiating learning to meet learner needs and preferences*.

The interconnected nature of the physical and digital experiences offered through embedding technology can also be enhanced by an interdisciplinary approach. In the case studies above, there are opportunities to make meaningful connections across subjects. Indeed, these are often required to make the most of the learning possibilities inherent in the activity. This can lead us towards moving from Science, Technology, Engineering and Mathematics (STEM) towards including the arts and addressing STEAM. Weaving together some or all of these subjects allows us to create connections for our pupils that see them working practically and creatively across several disciplines. One of the most exciting features of learning when art and design and digital technologies are combined is the collaboration between pupils in the same classroom and school, but going beyond this, across schools and in particular between schools in different countries. This supports us to make partnerships that explore cultures, interculturality and others' lives while engaging fully in the possibilities that the digital world can offer to artists, schools and their learners. In the Warwick Commission's blueprint for Britain's cultural and creative enrichment (2015, p. 15), Goal 4 was *a thriving digital cultural sphere that is open and available to all*. Using channels such as Skype and Google Hangouts, and initiatives such as eTwinning or Connecting Classrooms, along with collaborative digital tools that allow shared learning regardless of geographical distance, partnerships can lead to a greater understanding of cultures, and diverse and innovative ways of working in the creative arts.

References

Adams, J and Hiett, S (2012) The centrality of art, design and the performing arts to education. *IJADE*, 31(3): 218–20.

Craft, A (2013) Childhood, possibility thinking and wise, humanising educational futures. *International Journal of Educational Research*, 61: 126–34.

Department for Education (DfE) (2011) *Teachers' Standards Guidance for School Leaders, School Staff and Governing Bodies*. Available at: www.gov.uk/government/publications/teachers-standards (accessed 22 May 2017).

DfE (2013) *Art and Design Programmes of Study: Key Stage 1 and 2. National Curriculum in England*. Available at: www.gov.uk/government/publications/national-curriculum-in-england-art-and-design-programmes-of-study (accessed 22 May 2017).

DfE (2017) *Performance (P scale) Attainment Targets for Pupils with Special Educational Needs (SEN).* Available at: www.gov.uk/government/publications/p-scales-attainment-targets-for-pupils-with-sen (accessed 9 June 2017).

Edwards, J (2014a) *Teaching Primary Art.* Harlow: Pearson.

Edwards, J (2014b) Inspired by digital. *AD* magazine, NSEAD, autumn issue, 11: 24–5.

Edwards, J (2017) Crossing boundaries through digital learning. *AD Magazine, NSEAD.* Issue 20: 16–17.

Efland, A (2002) *Art and Cognition.* New York: Teachers College Press.

Eisner, E (2002) *The Arts and the Creation of Mind.* New Haven, CT: Yale University Press.

Fleming, M (2012) *The Arts in Education: An Introduction to Aesthetics, Theory and Pedagogy.* London: Routledge.

Gast, G (2012) *Effective Questioning and Talk in Art and Design.* Available at: www.nsead.org/downloads/ Effective_Questioning&Talk.pdf (accessed 25 May 2017).

Gast, G (2015) *Exploring and Developing the Spiritual, Moral, Social and Cultural Dimensions of Art and Design.* Available at : www.nsead.org/downloads/SMSC_in_art_and__design_2015.pdf (accessed 7 June 2017).

Heaton, R (n.d.) Digital art pedagogy in the United Kingdom. In: *International Encyclopedia of Art and Design Education.* London: Sage (in press).

Heaton, R (2014) Moving mindsets: Re-conceptualising the place of visual culture as multi-sensory culture in primary art education. *Canadian Review of Art Education*, 41(1): 77–96.

Hetland, L, Winner, E, Veenema, S and Sheridan, KM (2007) *Studio Thinking: The Real Benefits of Visual Arts Education.* New York: Teachers College Press.

Hickman, R and Heaton, R (2016) *Visual Art: The SAGE Handbook of Curriculum, Pedagogy and Assessment.* London: SAGE.

Lawton, PH (2014) The role of art education in cultivating community and leadership through creative collaboration. *Visual Inquiry: Learning and Teaching Art*, 3(3): 421–36.

Liu, GZ, Wu, NW and Chen, YW (2013) Identifying emerging trends for implementing learning technology in special education: A state-of-the-art review of selected articles published in 2008–12. *Research in Developmental Disabilities*, 34(10): 3618–28.

McLellan, R and Nicholl, B (2013) Creativity in crisis in Design & Technology: Are classroom climates conducive for creativity in English secondary schools? *Thinking Skills and Creativity*, 9: 165–85.

National College for Teaching and Leadership (NCTL) (2014) *National Award for Special Educational Needs Co-ordinator: Learning Outcomes.* Available at: www.gov.uk/government/publications/national-award-for-sen-co-ordination-learning-outcomes (accessed 22 May 2017).

National Society for Art and Design in Education (NSEAD) (2012) *The 21st Century Art and Design Primary Teacher.* Wiltshire: NSEAD. Available at: www.nsead.org/downloads/art_teacher_21st_century_primary.pdf (accessed 5 June 2017).

NSEAD (2014a) *A Framework for Progression, Planning for Learning, Assessment, Recording and Reporting.* Wiltshire: NSEAD.

NSEAD (2014b) *A Manifesto for Art, Craft and Design Education.* Wiltshire: NSEAD. Available at: www.nsead.org/downloads/NSEADManifesto-2014.pdf (accessed 5 June 2017).

NSEAD (2016) *The National Society for Art and Design in Education Survey Report 2015–2016.* Wiltshire: NSEAD. Available at: www.nsead.org/downloads/survey.pdf (accessed 6 June 2017).

Ní Bhroin, M (2015) Teachers' experiences with formative assessment in primary art education. *Visual Inquiry*, 4(1): 33–51.

Nilson, C, Fetherston, CM, McMurray, A and Fetherston, T (2013) Creative arts: An essential element in the teacher's toolkit when developing critical thinking in children. *Australian Journal of Teacher Education*, 38(7): 1–18.

Patton, R and Buffington, M (2016) Keeping up with our students: The evolution of technology and standards in art education. *Arts Education Policy Review*, 117(3): 1–9.

Pooley, E and Rowell, A (2016) *Studying Craft 16: Trends in Craft Education and Training* (3rd edn). Crafts Council. Available at: www.craftscouncil.org.uk/content/files/Studying_Craft_16.pdf (accessed 7 June 2017).

Robins, C (2016) Who assesses the assessors? Sustainability and assessment in art and design education. *International Journal of Art & Design Education*, 35(3): 348–55.

Training and Development Agency (TDA) (2010) *Including Pupils with SEN and/or Learning Disabilities in Primary Art and Design.* Manchester: TDA.

The Warwick Commission (2015) *Enriching Britain: Culture, Creativity and Growth.* Coventry: University of Warwick.

Wegerif, RB (2012) *Dialogic: Education for the Internet Age.* London: Routledge.

Chapter 9

PSHE

CLAIRE GUTHRIE, IN COLLABORATION WITH DALRY PRIMARY SCHOOL, NORTH AYRSHIRE

Introduction

This chapter examines how primary teachers and Special Educational Needs Coordinators (SENCOs) might integrate technology in Personal, Social and Health Education (PSHE) lessons for children in the Primary stages. Practical guidance is offered on employing technology in the PSHE curriculum at Key Stages 1 and 2. A diverse range of technologies is explored, including assistive or inclusive technologies as well as more general educational technologies. Through case studies and examples, this chapter will show how technology can enhance the development of pupils' life skills, and provide specialised support to groups and individuals where needed.

A range of themes are explored including:

- technology supporting life skills within the community;

- games-based learning and leisure;

- creating social stories to assist with social and emotional understanding;

- independent living skills.

In the broadest sense, PSHE can be seen as a 'curriculum for life'. Through a well-delivered PSHE curriculum, children are equipped with the knowledge and skills to: make positive life choices which support health and well-being; stay safe and manage risk; and be enterprising and effective citizens who understand their own needs as well as the needs of others. PSHE can be taught as 'stand-alone' lessons, or integrated with topic work – e.g. teaching about healthy eating while looking at the diet of the Tudors. Given the flexible nature of PSHE within schools, opportunities abound for using technology to enrich and enhance learning.

Learning objectives

By the end of this chapter you should be able to:

- understand the PSHE curriculum;
- promote the development of life skills through the use of inclusive technologies;
- establish a positive and inclusive classroom culture in which technology is used to enhance pupils well-being and understanding of self and others.

Links to Teachers' Standards

Adapt teaching to respond to the strengths and needs of all pupils

- Know when and how to differentiate appropriately, using approaches which enable pupils to be taught effectively.
- Have a secure understanding of how a range of factors can inhibit pupils' ability to learn, and how best to overcome these.
- Have a clear understanding of the needs of all pupils, including those with special educational needs; those of high ability; those with English as an additional language; those with disabilities; and be able to use and evaluate distinctive teaching approaches to engage and support them.

Manage behaviour effectively to ensure a good and safe learning environment

- Manage classes effectively, using approaches which are appropriate to pupils' needs in order to involve and motivate them

Part 2

- Treat pupils with dignity, building relationships rooted in mutual respect, and at all times observing proper boundaries appropriate to a teacher's professional position.
- Have regard for the need to safeguard pupils' well-being, in accordance with statutory provisions.
- Show tolerance of and respect for the rights of others.
- Not undermining fundamental British values, including democracy, the rule of law, individual liberty and mutual respect, and tolerance of those with different faiths and beliefs.

Links to National Curriculum Programmes of Study

- PSHE is a non-statutory subject. To allow teachers the flexibility to deliver high-quality PSHE we consider it unnecessary to provide new standardised frameworks or programmes of study.
- We expect schools to use their PSHE education programme to equip pupils with a sound understanding of risk and with the knowledge and skills necessary to make safe and informed decisions.

Reflective question

- What guidance is available to schools in teaching PSHE?

The Department for Education advises that *all schools should teach PSHE, drawing on good practice* (gov.uk, 2017a). Although PSHE is a non-statutory subject, schools in England are encouraged to develop their own curriculum – responsibility for planning and delivery of lessons is given to teachers who are deemed as being in the best position to know their pupils and their needs. The PSHE Association is grant funded by the government to support teachers in this task and has developed an on-line educational programme of study for Key Stages 1–5 (pshe-association.org.uk, 2017).

Assessment

For children who cannot access the National Curriculum due to Special Educational Needs (SEND), the P-scales offer a framework for monitoring success and achievement (gov.uk, 2017b). The P-scales are a list of performance indicators that are below Key Stage 1 of the National Curriculum. Their aim is to ensure that children with SEND show progress and achieve in accordance with their abilities. Progress in PSHE can be tracked using these scales.

Reflective question

- How do you integrate technology in lessons when teaching PSHE?

Useful technologies in teaching PSHE

The following section discusses a range of technologies that may be used in teaching PSHE in the primary classroom and beyond.

Augmented Reality (AR)

Skilfully employing augmented reality to help achieve learning objectives in PSHE can ensure that lessons leap beyond the everyday, energising and enthusing a captive classroom audience. There are many engaging augmented reality apps available that lend themselves easily to classroom and leisure use.

Augmented reality gives children the opportunity to interact with virtual objects that appear as if in the real world. Digital information – animated figures, videos, pictures, text, audio – is 'revealed' through a device's camera 'augmenting' or adding to the real world.

Pokémon GO

Pokémon GO (Niantic Inc., 2017) is perhaps the most widely known augmented reality mobile game, which caused a craze when it became available to the market in 2016. The excitement and fun, as well as the educational benefits of Pokémon GO, can be employed within the classroom and local environment. Players design an avatar, which appears on a map and follows the geographical location of the player's device. Through the avatar, players seek Pokémon – digital characters – which appear in the real world. GPS maps displayed on screen via the device camera, allow players to collect Pokémon, find PokéStops and PokéGyms.

Pokémon GO offers children a potentially rich opportunity to go beyond the walls of the classroom (devices need a cellular data plan when outwith Wi-Fi range). The everyday world takes on a new dimension as Pokémon appear on screen, as if in the real world, while children work together to stay safe, take turns, meet others on the same quest and see their neighbourhood in a new light – all while being physically on the move.

eSafety considerations

When Pokémon GO first appeared there were newspaper reports describing injuries players received while roaming locations to find virtual creatures (Mail Online, 2016). Given the potential safety issues while playing Pokémon GO, an initial task might be to get pupils to highlight the risks (road safety, hazards, stranger danger) and create 'play safe' guidelines.

Pokémon GO engages children in the PSHE curriculum in several ways, including the following examples:

- physical activity/skill – walking to various locations to find Pokémon, developing hand-eye coordination;

- risk and safety – following GPS navigation in the local environment while avoiding hazards;

- digital citizenship – meeting other players on location, 'stranger danger';

- social learning – meeting others at PokéStops, playing with friends, sharing learning and knowledge.

Differentiation

It has been noted that some children with autism can benefit from the social communication and learning opportunities Pokémon GO provides, as can those with anxiety and low mood (abilitynet.org.uk, 2017). However, consideration may need to be given to children with SEND when playing a game that demands physical and visual skills. Children with mobility difficulties, for example, may need assistance or a planned route getting about to find Pokémons, while those with significant visual impairment may find navigating menus and striking Pokémon with Poké Balls a near impossible task. For the visually impaired child, creative alternatives such as using Pokémon figures and toy Poké Balls could be incorporated in the play to represent for the child what is happening on screen and maintain involvement and inclusion.

Aurasma

As mentioned, deploying augmented reality in the classroom is easier than might be thought – all that is needed is a device with an appropriate AR app installed. One such app, commonly used for creating AR experiences in the classroom is the free app Aurasma (Aurasma, 2016). Aurasma is simple to use on a basic level. An object or image from the real world is used as 'trigger' for an 'aura' to appear (an aura is the real-world image overlaid with a digital creation – e.g. video, audio, animation, etc. via a device's camera). Aurasma Studio (Aurasma, 2017) is the online version of the software which allows for easy Aura creation and sharing to multiple devices. Advanced features include creating Auras with many overlays, loading URLs as overlays, and so on. You can find Aurasma video tutorials online and a user guide within the app.

With Aurasma, PSHE lessons can instantly become innovative and creative. Examples of use include the following.

- Create an interactive wall on healthy eating for your classroom using 'auras' which come to life when a device locates the 'trigger' image.

- Video record 'people who help us' speaking on video and overlay on an image of the person in an interactive book.

- Create a safety and protection 'trigger hunt' by 'tagging' related objects (first-aid box, extinguishers, fire blanket, push-bar exits, etc.) in the school environment which pupils need to locate to receive 'aura' messages. Auras can be simple or complex depending on the needs and ability of the group. Older children might create a 'trigger hunt' for another team to play.

VisionSim (Braille Institute, 2013) is an augmented reality app that simulates the effects of a visual impairment in the real word. This app can be used as a way of teaching older pupils about the experience of being visually impaired.

Virtual reality

Experiencing a virtual world is often described as 'immersive'; donning a virtual headset has the power to transport the user into an absorbing new reality. Virtual reality (VR) gives children the opportunity to experience new worlds and to interact within these worlds. The power of a VR educational experience is unleashed when learning objectives are met by engaging in a virtual world. Now that VR has reached the consumer market, applications, devices and headsets are available at a low cost.

Google Cardboard viewers, for example, combined with a device and the free Expeditions app (Google Inc., 2017) provide not only an affordable but also highly effective selection of virtual worlds for children to explore. The Expeditions app is used by both pupils and teacher, with the class teacher guiding and highlighting points of interest to children as they explore new worlds through their devices. The app is suited for individual, class or group use. Google Expeditions kits can be purchased for group and class use.

Children can choose from over 400 Expeditions on a wide range of topics from The Great Barrier Reef to Buckingham Palace. The Expeditions are multidisciplinary and lend themselves to integrated learning. In terms of the PSHE curriculum, children can journey through the human body using the collection of Expeditions on Human Anatomy, find out about disease control through Beating Ebola in Sierra Leone, and develop knowledge of difference and diversity through up-close knowledge of other cultures – for example, Girl Power to Beat Poverty in Bangladesh. Many expeditions are ideal for integrated projects, including World War I and II, and The Medieval Castle, which could lead to an exploration of human or children's rights. There are a number of expeditions that help develop empathy and understanding for different cultures – e.g. The Teepee, Out of Syria, and many more. A growing bank of lessons based on expeditions prepared by teachers for use in the classroom can be found online from the *Times Educational Supplement* (TES).

Virtual lessons truly have the potential to engage a child's sense of wonder; virtual reality offers children the chance to discover inaccessible or distant locations, and explore vistas and contexts that might never be seen in real life. For some children with SEND, virtual reality presents an opportunity to motivate and engage learners who are hard to reach, perhaps because of autism, disengagement or withdrawal. A child with autism can nurture a special interest through this technology; children with physical disabilities or health issues, who might experience limitations, can collect their packed lunch and set off on a virtual field trip of their own planning and choosing. For sighted children with SEND, VR has the potential to be liberating; pupils can explore new landscapes without physical limitations.

At the time of writing, the Google Pioneer Program (https://edu.google.com) offers free visits to schools. The program offers a chance to experience VR in the classroom with Google providing the kits (Asus smartphones, a tablet for the teacher to direct the tour, a router that allows Expeditions to run without an internet connection, as well as a library of over 100 virtual trips and Google Cardboard viewers) and the training for teachers to lead children through expeditions.

As virtual reality becomes widely available to mainstream markets, headsets, devices and apps are proliferating and educators have a growing array of options to choose from such as VR platforms like AltspaceVR (available for free on Daydream, Vive, Gear VR and Rift headsets) and Lecture VR (an initiative of Immersive VR Education).

Combining a VR headset with an aerial drone can enable the exploration of worlds and environments that might otherwise be outwith limits or out of bounds due to distance, physical limitations or other practical reasons. A VR headset paired with a drone, offers an immersive 360° first-person view (FPV), and adds a new dimension to exploring the playground or local park while on project work. Drones can also be used as a remote presence device potentially allowing a child with physical disabilities or health issues access to places otherwise out of bounds, such as an inaccessible school trip. Remote presence devices, such as the Double, have been on the market for a few years, allowing for a remote-controlled 'telepresence' on location, but requiring a smooth surface for stability. With drones, 'tele tourists' (May et al., 2017) can potentially travel the world from their home or classroom.

Social stories

A powerful way to deliver a message, for children and teachers alike, is through story making and telling. Ebooks on just about any PSHE topic can be found online through platforms such as iBooks or Kindle; there are also stories and story collections that can be purchased as apps and incorporated in lesson planning. Story creation apps can assist in producing stories through structured templates, image libraries, animated features, widgets, text to speech, audio recording, and so on. Technology can support teachers in creating Social Stories to help children gain understanding, skills and knowledge, and empower learners to tell stories about themselves, about their lives and communities, and to demonstrate what they have learned.

Carol Gray (http://carolgraysocialstories.com), a teacher of children with autism, evolved Social Stories as a social learning tool. Social Stories are carefully crafted narratives which describe a situation, skill or concept according to a set of research-based criteria. Gray outlines the science and art of creating Social Stories, in which crafting a Social Story is a defined process. Social Stories involve a patient, supportive and unassuming quality, and are described as a safe and meaningful exchange of information between the Author and intended Audience, a person with autism. For Gray, a Social Story can be screened to determine whether it is a true Social Story or not. Her work has spawned wide interest in Social Stories, including literature that reflects on the key principles of the approach, providing examples in use (Howley and Arnold, 2005), as well as a range of eBook and story creation tools that can be found online.

The StoryMaker for Social Stories (Handhold Adaptive®) app enables teachers to create social stories with pictures and text, add audio or text to speech, with the option to share books as PDF files or as print. The stories are intended for children with special needs – autism in particular – but not exclusively as children with Attention Deficit Hyperactivity Disorder (ADHD), Down's Syndrome, developmental delays, and so on may also benefit. The latest version of the app includes ten classic social stories by Carol Gray. All stories provided in the app can be customised, emailed and printed.

Differentiation

There is an extent to which social stories have become 'popularised'. As discussed, social stories can be beneficial for children with autism, but can also be adapted for use for children with ADHD, Down's Syndrome, developmental delays or for social skills training for groups and classes, and are invaluable as part of a PSHE toolbox. Thiemann and Goldstein (2001) investigated the effect of using written and pictorial cues with children with autism. Following the study, the authors concluded that intervention that combined pictorial and written text cues led to an improvement in baseline social communication skills for children with social impairments.

Social Stories Creator and Library (Touch Autism) is an app that, as the title suggests, enables the creation of social stories as well as providing a library of pre-made social story eBooks. eBook topics include *How to Calm Down*, *Making Conversation* and *Using and Sharing Money*, and can be purchased in topic bundles.

There are many apps that can be used for creating your own social stories on a PSHE theme. Puppet Pals (polishedplay.com, 2017), for example, equips children to tell simple animated stories with audio. Children choose their characters, a background (from stage-set backgrounds or uploaded photos) and have great fun composing and telling their story. Topics can be given that are PSHE themed – e.g. The Healthy Knight and How the Wicked Witch got Tamed.

Book Creator for iPad (Red Jumper Limited) is a story creation tool that combines visuals with text, allowing for the addition of video, music and voice. Children can read their final book creations in iBooks and share them through various methods including via AirDrop.

When it comes to the creation of animated stories in the classroom, StikBot Animations present the tools to make this job easy. StikBots are surprisingly inspiring articulated plastic figures with suction cups on hands and feet enabling a variety of poses. Combine StikBots with a device, the free Zing StikBot Studio (Zing Global Ltd) app and even a green screen, and children have their own animation studio at their fingertips. Pupils can use photos to form a background, add narration, music and titles to create a quality production for sharing with others.

StikBots are 'neutral' characters with limited expression. They may help some children process and manage their feelings and emotions through role play in which behaviours can be reviewed and modified with careful guidance. For example, children can produce a StikBot animation to resolve a playground conflict, to explore feelings and behaviour, or as a tool to express their own personal needs and views. Pupils can integrate their own favourite character figures to add a personal touch to a story or to help a child express him/herself. Animations can be shared via AirDrop, email, Cloud service, or published online on social media or YouTube. StikBot plastic figures even have an application beyond animations; for children who need to fidget constantly, a StikBot in hand may aid concentration.

Case study 1: StikBot

Sophie is in a mainstream Primary 4 class and has been referred for further assessment for Autism Spectrum Disorder (ASD). She has difficulty sharing with her peers and the class teacher believes this stems from Sophie's difficulties in social communication. The class teacher decides to introduce StikBot animation to Sophie and a partner. The learning objective is for the children to demonstrate the concept of sharing through a stop-motion animation film.

Stikbot figures come with a free Stikbot Studio app which is simple to navigate, enabling stop-motion animations to be created relatively effortlessly. A green screen and camera stand can be used to aid the film production process and come as a pack with the Stikbot Zanimation Studio. Animal StikBots are available for purchase and personal character figures or plasticine models can also play a part.

Impact on learning

Each pupil is given a figure and a ball of plasticine to share. Sophie is given her favourite Disney character figure Elsa to ensure engagement. The children are told that the figures do not know how to share. They will tell the story of how figures learned to share. Once the story has been developed, the teacher led the children through the sequence of activities to make the film. Replaying the completed film reinforces the concept of sharing to the children. The *How Elsa and the StickBot Learned to Share* film can also be screened for others (with or without popcorn) and posted on the school's YouTube channel or Facebook page.

Figure 9.1   Stikbot Zanimation Studio (source: Zing, 2017)

Figure 9.2 Stikbot Animation Image (source: Claire Guthrie, 2017)

Boardmaker Studio (www.boardmakeronline.com) software is a handy all-in-one tool that easily supports the creation of accessible learning and teaching resources. A popular classroom tool, Boardmaker Studio, provides a symbol library that can support the creation of a range of resources including Social Stories as well as songs, menus, signs, books, worksheets, calendars, timetables, to do lists, communication boards, and so on. A 30-day free trial is available from the producers Mayer-Johnson.

Teachers can also find free symbol and template libraries online to support resource creation. Picto-Selector (www.pictoselector.eu, 2017) contains over 2,800 simple yet effective black-and-white images with supporting text that can be translated into a number of languages. Created for children with autism, this resource is also a great communication aid for children with English as a Second or Other Language (ESOL) needs in the early stages. ConnectABILITY (connectability.ca, 2017) likewise provides a symbol library with templates and a facility to add text in order to create support for children on task and in learning new skills or concepts.

Gesture-based technology

All children and young people are entitled to an appropriate education, one that is appropriate to their needs, promotes high standards and the fulfilment of potential (gov.uk, 2017c).

Gesture-based computing uses body movements or voice to control applications rather than a keyboard, mouse or other input device. Inclusive provision is made easier with gesture-based computing as the range of input methods available can give children independent access to digital resources for learning and leisure.

Gesture-responsive technologies include:

- tablet devices that rely on hand or finger movements such as swiping, tapping and stretching for navigation and control;

- Eyegaze control systems that give full PC control through tracking the pupil movement;

- motion sensors from the world of gaming such as Xbox Kinect or Nintendo Wii remote controller that detect body movements that are translated into action on screen, including the Leap Motion controller for hand and finger tracking;

- voice recognition applications, and personal assistants such as Apple's Siri which enable users to control mobile iOS devices through speech.

Gesture-based technology is often described as 'intuitive'. Improvised gestures can be fun when exploring the effect of body movements on screen or exploring a new tablet device. However, it is important to remember that despite many children being skilled in the use of mobile devices, deeper or hidden features may need to be taught – e.g. three-finger tapping to turn on magnification in iOS devices, or learning voice recognition commands to ensure effective results. Ballyland software is designed for children who are blind or have low vision. Ballyland Magic app (www.sonokids.org) for iPad is a fun, educational app that teaches voice-over and foundation gestures to help navigate voice-over. It also helps support the parents and teachers of a child with visual impairment to gain an understanding of voice-over.

Case study 2: Prodigi Connect 12

Roddy is six years old and uses the Prodigi Connect 12 in class to help with a range of magnification tasks including close-up and distance viewing. Roddy has a visual impairment and used the camera on an iPad in Primary 1 as a magnifier, but his teacher recognised that he needed extra support when it came to writing in Primary 2. With the help of his Visual Impairment teacher, the Prodigi Connect 12 was identified as a magnifier that would enable Roddy to undertake most visual tasks around the classroom with comfort and ease.

The Prodigi Connect 12 is a product supplied by Humanware comprising a Samsung Android tablet and magnification app, and a detachable camera for distance viewing attached by means of a snake clamp to the bespoke stand supporting the device.

Impact on learning

Roddy can now write under the tablet using the magnification app, viewing his magnified writing on the tablet screen which is positioned for ergonomic ease. He can cut neatly with scissors using the same method, as well as examine pictures up close and add detail to the plasticine models he enjoys making with tools. The distance magnifier, which attaches to Roddy's desk with a snake clamp, can magnify the Smartboard and wall posters. Roddy uses distance magnification to read the words for the week list from the Smartboard on his tablet and can see a visitor's face as they arrive in the classroom. Videos and films as well as content for sharing on the teacher's laptop can be shared via Wi-Fi directly to Roddy's tablet using the TeamViewer app (TeamViewer, 2017).

Figure 9.3   Prodigi Connect 12 (source: Humanware, 2016)

Eyegaze

Ground-breaking advancements in technology such as Eyegaze control systems can give a child access to the digital world, giving them a sense of freedom and autonomy, as well as many new and exciting opportunities to learn and play. Like virtual reality, Eyegaze has become more affordable and is increasingly prevalent in education. Eyegaze works by tracking the learner's pupil; as the child holds their gaze on an on-screen item for a pre-set time, the item is selected. For some children, Eyegaze requires less effort than a switch (an alternative PC access method) and can help a child with physical difficulties to achieve their best.

For children with no or limited speech, Eyegaze gives access to Augmented and Alternative Communication (AAC), which are powerful communication systems using software such as Grid 2 (Smartbox Assistive Technology). In basic terms, Grid 2 presents vocabulary grids with words, pictures (or both) as well as text-based communication. Grid 2 is not only a fast and accurate communication tool, but also a computer access program.

Eyegaze devices such as myGaze® Assistive 2 (Visual Interaction), which tracks eye movement, combined with an access program such as EyeMouse Play (Visual Interaction), which gives PC control, can offer children with limited motor control the power of a mouse. Children can gain the freedom and autonomy to navigate the operating system, and access learning and leisure tools. Programs such as Look to Learn (Smartbox Assistive Technology) offer fun educational activities which help children develop their skills in using the technology. Jackson Pollock painting (JacksonPollock. org, 2017) allows children freedom of artistic expression. Eyegaze tracking can be used as an assessment tool for teachers. Look to Learn software, for example, gives teachers a visual tracking analysis that shows the child's focus and engagement with activities on screen, intended to inform lesson planning.

Kinect

Software developers are tapping into the power of educational or therapeutic games to support a range of needs. In Zakari's (2017) review of 40 'serious games' for autistic children, she notes that research has shown the effectiveness of playing games on mobile devices for children with Autism Spectrum Disorder to help express feelings and improve their level of engagement with others.

Somantics software (Cariad Interactive, 2017) has been developed at Cardiff Metropolitan University as a resource to engage, stimulate and encourage creative movement in children with ASD. The software is free, can be downloaded online and used on a PC, Mac or as an iPad app. Pair Somantics with an Xbox Kinect (the motion sensor device that comes with an Xbox) and then link to an overhead projector; the Kinect senses a child's movement and translates this via the software to projected graphics on the wall. Somantics is designed to engage children visually and physically, thereby promoting self-awareness, confidence and communication. Through body movements, children can paint the wall with colour, create sparkles, and so on. Although the app is intended for use with children with ASD, it can be used in the gym to stimulate creative movement or as a colourful addition for an expressive dance activity, especially for a deaf child who may benefit from the visual support. Children who find it hard to move or to express themselves through their bodies, or who have limited movement may enjoy the sense of play and exploration this tool brings. As soon as you realise your movement has an effect upon the visual display, it's hard to resist exploring the effects you can create. There is also an iPad version of the software.

Soundbeam 5 (The Soundbeam Project) is a music-making program that also uses sensors to translate body movement into sound for all ages and abilities. The program was initially developed for dancers, although it is packaged for use in special education. A child in a wheelchair, for example, can choose a sound using a switch, move through the 'soundbeam' in their wheelchair and effect changes to a sound, thereby creating music through motion. The program measures how the child moves and how fast, and matches that to sounds like an 'invisible keyboard'. The program also includes a sound library, which can support story telling and drama performances, and even adds a new dimension to movement in the gym (e.g. scary sounds).

Leap Motion's Controller is a small peripheral device that allows for 3D tracking of hand and finger movements. The controller is available for Mac and PC, and offers a new and experimental way to interface with a computer. The device can be used with a range of free and paid apps that can be purchased on the Air Space Store. Children can use learned gestures to navigate the computer, fly through maps on Google Earth, or paint in the air with tailor-made apps such as Art Kit – Fledgling Edition (Angry Penguin, 2017). The Leap Motion Controller can also be used with a virtual reality headset allowing users to *leap into virtual reality with your bare hands* (Leap Motion, 2017).

Reflective question

- How can independent living aids be incorporated into PSHE lesson planning?

Integral to the PSHE curriculum is the teaching of independent living or 'life skills' enabling children to become resilient and confident in managing day-to-day activities and tasks as they move towards adulthood. In the classroom, paying attention to what a child can do, while keeping a focus on building self-esteem and a sense of achievement, can be more important than understanding a condition or impairment. How we approach daily living tasks depends on the skills and abilities we have; choosing what colour of jumper to wear, for example, is a different process for a blind or a sighted child. From making music to pouring a drink, there is a huge range of daily tasks and activities that technology can help with. For a child with SEND, assistive technology can unleash hidden potential, affording the child a much needed sense of autonomy and control that demonstrates their ability to be independent of the adults and carers around.

Children can gain a strong sense of what difference and inclusion mean by seeing the range of technological aids and adaptations manufactured to improve the quality of and independence in people's lives. An enterprising PSHE lesson could involve children researching and designing an aid for an elderly person, a homeless person or someone with a disability. Real life examples include recording pens, robotic cats, 'Cloud Grannies' and a simplified tablet interface. The children can develop 'prototypes' and marketing materials to appeal to their intended audience.

Technology can open up new worlds for children and it doesn't need to be cutting-edge to be effective; a tool as simple as a Talking Tin can be used to take a recorded message to the school office, giving a mute child an important role in school life. Talking Tins are coloured digital recording devices that can be secured to tins or other containers by magnets or straps. The device is rewritable and 'speaks' to identify the contents of the container. Talking Tins offer wider potential in the Primary classroom for creative play and learning; music, sounds (doorbell, rustling leaves, etc.) and speech can be recorded and the devices can be used as part of project work or language activities. Storytelling can be enhanced, displays can 'speak', and activity start and finish times can be announced by recorded sound.

Liquid level indicators, designed for the visually impaired to safely identify when a cup or container is full, offer another versatile tool for exploratory play and learning. Try including a liquid level indicator at the water table to gauge when a container is full of liquid, in the home corner for younger children or for managing liquid volume in experiments. Through deploying inclusive solutions in the classroom, all children learn that there are many ways to solve a problem and that people have varying needs.

Talking Clocks are useful for those with visual impairment and can help all children in learning to tell the time. Both digital and analogue clocks are available for purchase through a number of websites. LookTel Money Reader (IPPLEX, 2011), an app developed to speak the value of paper notes for those with sight loss, is an interesting way for sighted children in the early stages to learn about money and the power of technology to assist in daily life. At the same time, it has more serious application for the visually impaired child. The LookTel Recognizer (IPPLEX, 2011) app can also be both fun and educational in the home corner – sighted children can make a library of kitchen items with audio descriptions for others to 'recognise' through the device's camera.

Another aid for developing independence and life skills for visually impaired children is the Penfriend 2 Labeller. Penfriend can label anything and everything through digital voice recording. The pen has tactile operating buttons in high-contrast yellow and comes with labels. To make voice recordings, touch the sticker labels with the pen, then play back voice labels by retouching the sticker with the pen. Young children who are learning to read and write may find the speech support offered by this tool supportive in the classroom, as will children with ESOL.

Last but not least are switches. Switches are an access method developed for people who have limited motor control and can be used in the Primary classroom in a variety of ways. Put simply, switches complete an electrical circuit in order to activate another powered device. Like Eyegaze, switches can offer independence and autonomy through access to computers, communication systems, and also switch-accessible toys, page-turners and potentially home appliances, and powered wheelchairs. There are a variety of types of switch that can be used with learners; these include voice-activated switches, large or small buttons, sip/puff, pressure-activated switches, movement-activated sensor switches, and so on.

Scaffolding learning

Scaffolding learning about switches for a child with limited motor control allows the child's knowledge to develop in stages: beginning with operating responsive toys, building to environmental control systems at home (e.g. door and window openers, turning on lamps and lighting) through to full computer control, and so on. Once again, all children can learn through the use of switches in the classroom. Children learn not only about alternative access methods, but also about the need for independence, power and autonomy in all our lives in education and at home.

Summary and Key Points

This chapter has introduced a range of technological resources and solutions that promote inclusion and support children in understanding diversity. An important theme in the PSHE curriculum is teaching children about difference, equality and rights. From virtual field trips to new lands and cultures, to the use of a simple switch device to set a battery-operated toy in motion, technology can help a child expand his or her horizons and understand the differences between people. Technology can also engage learners in new and interesting ways. Somantics offers disengaged children the opportunity to interact with visual displays through movement, potentially opening a door to further learning experiences. As discussed, a proliferation of educational apps can be used in PSHE to promote health and well-being, teach a social skill, or help a child understand safety and risk. Teachers are in the fortunate position of being able to tap into a rich treasure chest of digital resources that can enhance storytelling, 'speak' displays and ensure that games become integral to learning. Providing experience of independent living aids and alternative access methods in the classroom environment is fertile ground for children to learn about autonomy and independence. Through employing inclusive solutions in the classroom, teachers can demonstrate to pupils that there are many solutions to a problem, while emphasising the importance of focusing on ability.

References

abilitynet.org.uk (2017) Pokémon Go: Are incense and Street View the key to more inclusivity for disabled people? Available at: www.abilitynet.org.uk/news-blogs/pok%C3%A9mon-go-are-incense-and-street-view-key-more-inclusivity-disabled-people (accessed 8 June 2017).

Angry Penguin (2017) Art Kit – Fledgling Edition (1.1.1) (mobile app) (accessed 8 June 2017).

Assistive Technology Ltd. Look to Learn (computer program). Available at: https://thinksmartbox.com/product/look-to-learn (accessed 8 June 2017).

Aurasma (2016) Aurasma (5.1.2) (mobile app) (accessed 8 June 2017).

Braille Institute (2013) VisionSim (3.0.1) (mobile app) (accessed 8 June 2017).

Cariad Interactive (2017) Somantics. Available at: http://cariadinteractive.com/somantics (accessed 27 February 2017).

carolgraysocialstories.com (2017) What is a Social Story? Available at: http://carolgraysocialstories.com/social-stories/what-is-it (accessed 27 February 2017).

connectability.ca (2017) Visuals Engine|ConnectABILITY. Available at: http://connectability.ca/visuals-engine (accessed 27 February 2017).

edu.google.com (2017) Expeditions Pioneer Program – Google. Available at: https://edu.google.com/intl/en_uk/pioneer-program (accessed 8 June 2017).

Google Inc. (2017) Expeditions (1.1.1) (mobile app) (accessed 8 June 2017).

Department for Education (DFE) (2017a) Personal, social, health and economic (PSHE) education. Available at: www.gov.uk/government/publications/personal-social-health-and-economic-education-pshe/personal-social-health-and-economic-pshe-education (accessed 27 February 2017).

Department for Education (DFE) (2017b) P scales: attainment targets for pupils with special educational needs. Available at: www.gov.uk/government/publications/p-scales-attainment-targets-for-pupils-with-sen (accessed 27 February 2017).

Department for Education, Department of Health (2017c) SEND code of practice: 0 to 25 years. Available at: www.gov.uk/government/publications/send-code-of-practice-0-to-25 (accessed 27 February 2017).

Handhold Adaptive®, LLC (2017) StoryMaker for Social Stories (4.4.2) (mobile app) (accessed 8 June 2017).

Howley, M and Arnold, E (2005) *Revealing the Hidden Social Code* (1st edn). London: Jessica Kingsley.

IPPLEX (2011) LookTel Money Reader (2.2) (mobile app) (accessed 8 June 2017).

IPPLEX (2013) LookTel Recogniser (1.3) (mobile app) (accessed 8 June 2017).

JacksonPollock.org (2017) "Jackson Pollock" by Miltos Manetas, original design by Stamen, press any key to start. Available at: www.JacksonPollock.org (accessed 28 February 2017).

Leap Motion (2017) Leap Motion. Available at: www.leapmotion.com (accessed 8 June 2017).

Mail Online (2016) How to avoid getting injured playing Pokemon Go. Available at: www.dailymail.co.uk/health/article-3696086/From-sunburn-aching-legs-blisters-doctors-reveal-5-common-Pokemon-injuries-avoid-them.html (accessed 27 February 2017).

May, K, May, K and May, K (2017) 5 new technologies that help disabled and bedridden people experience the world again. TED Blog. Available at: http://blog.ted.com/5-telepresence-technologies-that-have-emerged-since-henry-evans-ted-talk (accessed 8 June 2017).

Mayer-Johnson. Boardmaker. Available at: www.boardmakeronline.com (accessed 28 February 2017).

Niantic Inc. (2017) Pokemon GO (1.33.4) (mobile app) (accessed 8 June 2017).

Picto-Selector. Home – Picto-Selector. Available at: www.pictoselector.eu (accessed 27 February 2017).

Polished Play, LLC (2017) Puppet Pals (5.1.7) (mobile app) (accessed 8 June 2017).

PSHE Association (2017) Programme of Study for PSHE Education (Key stages 1–5)|PSHE Association. Available at: www.pshe-association.org.uk/curriculum-and-resources/resources/programme-study-pshe-education-key-stages-1%E2%80%935 (accessed 27 February 2017).

Red Jumper Limited (2017) Book Creator (5.1.1) (mobile app) (accessed 8 June 2017).

Smartbox Assistive Technology Ltd. The Grid 2 (computer program). Available at: https://think.com/product/the-grid-2 (accessed 8 June 2017).

Sonokids (2017) Ballyland Magic (1.0.5) (mobile app) (accessed 8 June 2017).

Soundbeam Project, The. Soundbeam 6 (computer program). Available at: www.soundbeam.co.uk/soundbeam-6-product-page (accessed 8 June 2017).

studio.aurasma.com (2017) Aurasma. Available at: https://studio.aurasma.com/landing (accessed 9 June 2017).

TeamViewer (2017) TeamViewer (12.1) (mobile app) (accessed 8 June 2017).

Thiemann, K and Goldstein, H (2001) Social stories, written text cues, and video feedback: effects on social communication of children with autism. *Journal of Applied Behavior Analysis*, 34(4): 425–46.

Touch Autism (2017) Social Stories Creator and Library (5.1.7) (mobile app) (accessed 8 June 2017).

Visual Interaction. myGaze® Assistive 2 – Eye Tracker and EyeMouse Play (computer program). Available at: www.dyslexic.com/product/mygaze-assistive-2/ (accessed 8 June 2017).

Zakari, H (2017) A Review of Serious Games for Children with Autism Spectrum Disorders (ASD). Available at: www.researchgate.net/profile/Hanan_Zakari/publication/291345119_A_Review_of_Serious_Games_for_Children_with_Autism_Spectrum_Disorders_ASD/links/56a1168208ae24f62701ebce.pdf (accessed 27 February 2017).

Zing Global Ltd (2017) Zing Stikbot Studio (3.0.3) (mobile app) (accessed 8 June 2017).

INDEX

Entries in **bold type** indicate apps.